**DO NOT REMOVE
CARDS FROM POCKET**

Companions Along The Way

Ruth (Shick) Montgomery

COWARD, McCANN & GEOGHEGAN, INC.
New York

To my sister Margaret
and husband Bob
My frequent comrades
along the way

Contents

Foreword

The genesis of this book is rather intriguing, having sprung into being either through a remarkable series of coincidences or by a sudden burst of mental telepathy. Readers of my previous books are aware that each morning at the same hour I sit at the typewriter and close my eyes, while a mysterious spirit who calls himself Lily apparently directs my fingers on the keyboard to bring information from the world beyond the grave.

Lily began his daily "appearances" in 1960 shortly after Arthur Ford, the famous American medium, encouraged me to develop automatic writing, and within a few months Lily reported that a group of twelve was now working with him on the project. The writing continued intermittently for eleven years until, the day following his fatal heart attack, Arthur Ford joined the sessions. Then, invariably starting the morning sessions with the words, "Ruth, this is Lily, Art, and the Group," the spirit guides began dictating material about the continuing stages of eternal life, published in 1971 under the title *A World Beyond*.

After completing that absorbing project, the Guides began writing about Creation, the advent of man on the earth, and the hierarchy of angels, until one day in early 1973 they abruptly shifted subject matter to write about the recruitment of His disciples by Jesus of Nazareth. Two days later, selecting at random from a large stack of unopened fan mail, I read a letter from an unknown reader who signed herself Marilee (Mrs. John Warren) Beach of Mount Kisco, New York, and wrote:

"Ever since you started writing, I have been one of your avid readers. Recently I read *A World Beyond* and found it absolutely fascinating, especially the statement that in a previous life you were a sister of Lazarus. Would you ever consider pursuing this, and possibly writing a book about the other sister of Lazarus?"

The idea had not occurred to me, but perhaps the Guides had read or inspired Mrs. Beach's letter, because the next morning they began our session by writing, "That will then be our project, to bring the story of the other sister of Lazarus, namely *YOU*. Arthur [Ford] will be of inestimable help, since he was with you at that time, and we will probe the akashic records for your own record in that period and time."

Each day thereafter the narrative continued as recorded in this book, and within a week it became apparent that the material should be of general interest, since it primarily concerned unknown facets in the life and ministry of Jesus. I therefore telephoned Patricia Soliman, my executive editor at Coward, McCann & Geoghegan, who exclaimed, "I've been intending to call you, because I have an idea for your next book."

Laughingly interrupting, I said, "First let me tell you what I'm writing now." I then told her about the letter from Mrs. Beach, who wanted to know more about the Palestinian incarnation in which Arthur Ford seemed to have been my father, and of the Guides' willingness to comply. There was a stunned silence, until Patricia gasped, "I have goose pimples! I was planning to suggest that you write about some of the previous incarnations you and Arthur Ford have shared." She explained that she had long been tantalized by a statement of mine in *A World*

Beyond: "Arthur has, of course, written about numerous other lives of mine and his, and of our previous contacts with some of the relatives and friends now living." But I had not elaborated on them. Now, two years later, Patricia was suddenly eager for me to do so. Thus it would seem that she, Mrs. Beach, and the Guides were at least temporarily operating on the same wavelength.

In *A World Beyond* I recounted a curious series of circumstances tending to indicate that in one of my past lives I had been a sister of Lazarus, Martha, and Mary, although the Bible makes no mention of such a person. To recapitulate: During several of my morning meditations in 1967 I seemed to relive a childhood period in Bethlehem, when I saw a brilliant star and knew that a baby had been born nearby. I watched some exotically dressed men arrive on camels to see the baby, and when I later heard that it was going to be bathed in a pool somewhere between Bethlehem and Jerusalem, I begged my father to let me follow the crowd that was going to the ceremony. He at first demurred, but I pleaded so desperately that at last we started down the road together, and as I slipped my little hand in his, I knew that he was the same soul as Arthur Ford, although there was no physical resemblance.

Later, while gathering material for *Here and Hereafter,* I submitted to hypnosis by a noted woman scientist whom I called Jane Winthrop, to protect her privacy. One of the lives that I seemingly tapped into was that same incarnation in Palestine, but this time I was a young matron whose husband violently disapproved of my interest in the teachings of Jesus. Under hypnosis I reenacted a scene in which I fled into the desert, abandoning husband and baby, to hear Jesus preach, and afterward I went to the house of Lazarus, whom I "knew" to be my brother. On being brought out of trance, I was deeply puzzled by the latter scene, because since Martha and Mary were both "there," I could not have been either sister.

I told no one of these experiences, but shortly after publication of *Here and Hereafter* in 1968, a man unknown to me wrote from Utah that while reading the book he experienced a "psychic flash" that I had once been a sister of Lazarus.

A few weeks later, on impulse, I bought *The Aquarian Gospel of Jesus the Christ*, after noting on the flyleaf that it claimed to have been dictated before 1907 by a discarnate who identified himself only as Levi. Since it was written in Biblical style, divided into chapter and verse, I read only a small portion each day until, to my astonishment, my eyes fell on these words:

"The evening came; the multitudes were gone, and Jesus, Lazarus, and his sisters Martha, Ruth and Mary, were alone. And Ruth was sore distressed. Her home was down in Jericho; her husband was the keeper of an inn; his name was Asher-ben. Now, Asher was a Pharisee of strictest mien and thought, and he regarded Jesus with disdain. And when his wife confessed her faith in Christ, he drove her from his home." The succeeding events as recounted by Levi neatly dovetailed with those I had experienced while under hypnosis, and after Arthur Ford's death in January, 1971, he "verified" that life of mine in Palestine, saying of himself, "I was the father of the brood."

Now, in this book he and the other Guides go into infinitely greater detail, recounting many heretofore-unknown incidents in the life of Jesus, the Holy Family, and others who are mentioned in the New Testament. This material was dictated through my typewriter during a period of four months, and not until the Guides finished did I seek to compare it with New Testament accounts or with those psychically received from Levi or through the great seer Edgar Cayce.

Biblical scholars agree that the four Gospels were largely written by men who had not been eyewitnesses to the events that transpired many decades earlier, and each account differs in some respects from the others. In like manner, Edgar Cayce while in trance sometimes contradicted his own previous utterances concerning the lifetime of Jesus, just as some of the material from my Guides conflicts with that of Cayce and Levi. Yet I am more impressed by the remarkable similarities than by the divergencies, because lawyers aver that no two eyewitnesses to an event give identical accounts.

If Lazarus indeed had a sister named Ruth, Edgar Cayce made no mention of her. This is understandable, because the non-Biblical characters he identified while in trance were said to have been previous incarnations of those for whom he was then giving life readings in Virginia Beach, and he was never asked whether there were other members of Lazarus' family. I was not privileged to have had a reading by Mr. Cayce or to have known him. The Guides, in explaining why Ruth was "left out of the Good Book," declared that since she was not there when Lazarus was raised from the dead, and was not living in his house, "there was no reason to mention her."

I have no way of knowing whether the soul that I now am once occupied the body of another Ruth in Palestine. I know only that on a visit to the Holy Land in January, 1963, long before I believed in reincarnation, I felt so peculiarly drawn to Jericho, the Dead Sea area, and Bethany that I repeatedly upset my planned itinerary to return to those sites. This fact certainly establishes no proof of what the Guides have written about that long-ago period, but the events that I "saw" while under hypnosis by Jane Winthrop are far more vivid to me now than most remembrances of my childhood.

The life readings given by Edgar Cayce while in trance stressed that groups of souls tend to reincarnate in cycles, meeting each other again and again in physical embodiment, being drawn together by some curious law of karmic attraction in order to work out mutual problems which had been left unresolved. But sometimes the purpose is simply to enjoy one another's company again or lend a hand, and this can explain the instant rapport that we feel with certain people on first meeting. Certainly that was my experience with Arthur Ford. I was a cynical newspaper columnist and he had the offbeat calling of a medium, yet he never seemed a stranger to me. Such adjectives as "enigmatic," "mysterious," "awe inspiring," and even "trickster" have been applied to him by many writers, but to me he was simply a friend who seemed almost like a member of the family.

Small wonder, if the material supplied me for this book is true! In it Arthur and the other Guides describe nine lives that he and I are said to have shared. Both in Palestine and in ancient Egypt at the time of Amenhotep IV and Nefertiti, Arthur Ford was allegedly my father, and in a Persian incarnation my son. Twice he was my younger brother, in the days of the great pharaoh builders and again in pre-Victorian England. In Tibet he was my guru, and in Greece my teacher. In still a third Egyptian life Arthur was a friend of my father's who served as mentor for my studies, and in Moab after the Exodus he was a friend who labored beside me in the fields.

Lily, my spirit pen pal since 1960 who has previously been so secretive about his earthly identity, now claims to have known me well in two of our previous incarnations, once as a friend and the other time as the father of Arthur Ford and me. In a third life shared with Arthur but not with me, Lily is identified as a figure of world renown.

Edgar Cayce said that before souls can complete the cycle of rebirths and step off the wheel of karma, they must have been both man and woman and have experienced life in various nationalities, races, and religions. I have seemingly had my share of these in the lives herein recorded, and although Lily and Arthur Ford inhabited solely male bodies in these accounts, both had many more lives than those they shared with me. And unquestionably all three of us will have to return many times before achieving the perfection which permits reunion with our Creator.

Why do most of us fail to recall our previous lives? It would be too great a burden to carry if our minds were clogged with so many memories. Thus, a kindly God gives us the opportunity to "start clean" each time and make of our lives what we will. None of us remembers his birth and babyhood in this lifetime, yet those events can be recalled to conscious memory under hypnosis, as medical doctors have repeatedly demonstrated. In fact, the intelligence branches of our armed services have often employed hypnosis to enable secret agents to recall observations made on spying trips that their conscious minds had overlooked.

Thus, if the theory of reincarnation is true, it seems logical to assume that episodes of previous lives can also be brought to present remembrance. Certainly there are hundreds of well-documented cases of small children who have had total recall of names, faces, and events suggestive of a previous lifetime, and whose assertions were subsequently proved correct when disinterested observers took them to the scene, where they identified strangers by name, accurately pointed out their former abode, described the layout of rooms before entering, and even secret hiding places. Many such instances have been detailed in *Here and Hereafter* and also in *Twenty Cases Suggestive of Reincarnation* by Dr. Ian Stevenson of the University of Virginia.

Among the best-known cases is that of a Hindu girl named Shanti Devi, who in 1937 at the age of four began discussing incidents of a previous life when she had been a Choban by caste. She claimed that her husband was Pt. Kedar Nath Chaubey, a cloth merchant who was living some distance away in Muttra, and she not only gave his address but also supplied so much information about her former home that her parents finally wrote to the name and address she furnished. Kedar Nath, who had since remarried, soon came to Delhi and Shanti immediately recognized the stranger as her "husband." He plied her with questions about himself and his home, and she answered all correctly, even describing the town where she had never been and a temple to which she had promised one hundred rupees, having buried the money under the floor of her house.

The four-year-old child, accompanied by fifteen investigators, then went to Muttra, where she accurately directed the driver to her former home at the end of a narrow lane, precisely describing the room arrangement before entering. She recognized her "father-in-law" without prompting and showed investigators where she had hidden the money for the temple. On digging a hole, they found a place for keeping valuables, but it was empty, and Kedar Nath admitted that after his first wife's death he had removed the money. Shanti then led the way to the home of her former "parents" and unhesitatingly embraced her "father" and "mother," although fifty people were present and some lovingly held out their arms in an attempt to trick her.

Reincarnation is the belief that each soul returns again and again to physical body, to atone for past errors and develop its full potential in preparation for ultimate reunion with God. This belief, older than recorded history, is accepted by approximately two-thirds of the world's population, particularly in the Orient but increasingly in the West. The Essenes, a Jewish sect recently made famous through discovery of the Dead Sea scrolls, and also the Biblical Pharisees believed in reincarnation, as did the followers of Jesus and the early Christians.

In Matthew 17:9–13 the disciples questioned Jesus about the Old Testament prophecy that Elias "must first come" before the Master, and Jesus replied: "Elias truly shall first come, and restore all things. But I say unto you, That

Elias is come already, and they knew him not, but have done unto him whatsoever they listed. Likewise shall also the Son of man suffer of them. Then the disciples understood that He spake unto them of John the Baptist." By the time Jesus uttered those words John the Baptist, who had come to prepare the way for Jesus, had been beheaded by Herod. Thus, it would be difficult to assign any meaning to Christ's words other than that John was the reincarnation of Elias, and the disciples so understood.

Matthew 16:13–14 records that when Jesus asked His disciples who men thought He was they responded: "Some say that thou art John the Baptist; some, Elias; and others, Jeremias, or one of the prophets." Is this not a reference to reincarnation? John 9:1–2 tells us: "And as Jesus passed by, he saw a man which was blind from his birth. And his disciples asked him, saying, Master, who did sin, this man, or his parents, that he was born blind?" Surely it is impossible for a man to sin before birth, unless he has lived before.

Early leaders of the Catholic Church continued to believe in reincarnation. Origen (A.D. 185–254), described by the *Encyclopaedia Britannica* as "the most distinguished and most influential of all the theologians of the ancient church, with the possible exception of Augustine," wrote in *De Principiis*, "The soul has neither beginning nor end. . . . Each soul . . . comes into this world strengthened by the victories or weakened by the defeats of its previous life. Its place in this world as a vessel appointed to honor or dishonor is determined by its previous merits or demerits. Its work in this world determines its place in the world which is to follow this . . . ."

In the *Confessions* of St. Augustine (A.D. 354–430) we read: "Did I not live in another body, or somewhere else, before entering my mother's womb?" In *Contra Academicos* Augustine further declares: "The message of Plato, the purest and most luminous in all philosophy, has at last scattered the darkness of error, and now shines forth mainly in Plotinus, a Platonist so like his master that one would think they lived together, or rather—since so long a period of time separates them—that Plato is born again in Plotinus." The *Encyclopaedia Britannica* states that "the soul," according to Plato, "is immortal, the number of souls fixed, and reincarnation regularly occurs."

Biblical scholars are agreed that early Church fathers had available to them numerous original texts from which to choose in assembling the New Testament, arbitrarily rejecting some and including others. Certainly it is true that deletions and additions were made in the material eventually selected. In the sixth century the Synod of Constantinople condemned the teachings of Origen, although Pope Vigilius of Rome snubbed the council, declining to attend even though he was in Constantinople at the time. Thereafter, it is a logical assumption that most references to reincarnation were deleted from the Bible. Suffice it to say that it is easier for religious leaders to discourage the vices of their constituents (and sell indulgences, as the Catholic Church used to do) if parishioners believe that this is their *only* lifetime in which to achieve salvation.

The concept of reincarnation has been taught by nearly all the world's great religions. It was a major precept of the Brahman faith many centuries before the birth of Buddha, who also espoused it. The Jewish Talmud states that the soul of Abel passed into the body of Seth and subsequently into that of Moses. The Koran of the Muslim faith declares: "God generates beings, and sends them back over and over again, until they return to Him."

Emperor Julian believed himself to be the reincarnation of Alexander the Great, and Napoleon repeatedly insisted that he was Charlemagne. Henry David Thoreau wrote that he recalled living in Judea at the time of Christ, that he knew the writer Hawthorne in a former life when they walked amid ruins of chariots, and that he remembered still another life as a shepherd in Assyria.

Those who saw the recent motion picture *Patton* witnessed the dramatic scene in which General George S. Patton, Jr., suddenly recalled a previous life as a Roman warrior. Harry H. Semmes in his book *Portrait of Patton* states that Patton personally told him about the incident in 1918, while both were serving with the tank corps in France. He relates that Patton, sent on a secret mission to a part of France unknown to him, had the eerie feeling that in a former existence he knew the area well, and he correctly pointed out the location of two ancient Roman camps, although neither could be glimpsed from where he stood. Later Patton wrote a long poem in which he enumerated some of his previous lives as a soldier.

Many other figures prominent in modern Western thought have written of their belief in reincarnation. Among the hundreds are Benjamin Franklin, Victor Hugo, Frederick the Great, Sir Arthur Conan Doyle, John Masefield, David Lloyd George, Arthur Schopenhauer, Spinoza, Harry Houdini, Louis Bromfield, Henry Ford, Hervey Allen, Jack London, Richard Wagner, Khalil Gibran, Louisa May Alcott, Ralph Waldo Emerson and his brother Charles, Dante Gabriel Rossetti, and Walt Whitman.

Thus, we are in good company in believing that we have lived and loved and died many times before and that our present embodiment is not likely to be our last. Obviously I lack proof of what "Lily, Art, and the Group" have written about the parallel lives Arthur Ford and I are said to have shared, but certainly they are not in the writing style I would have employed if I could have created them from imagination. In the Palestinian narrative which follows, the alleged third sister of Lazarus is referred to sometimes as Ruth and at other times as "you," and I have refrained from altering their manner of expression. The material usually seems to be a group effort, although occasionally Arthur Ford exuberantly takes over to write about himself in the first person as Jeremiah, the father of Ruth, Lazarus, Martha, and Mary.

The events as dictated to me do not always conform exactly to New Testament accounts, but in rereading the four Gospels after the Guides completed their work, I noticed that Matthew, Mark, Luke, and John are often at variance with each other. They do not even agree on the recruitment of the disciples. Further, modern translations made from the earliest available documents demonstrate numerous errors in the King James version. This is understandable when one considers that the original testaments were written in Aramaic and Hebrew, but translated into Greek, then Latin, and ultimately from these into modern languages.

It is also probable that I am an imperfect receiving instrument, unwittingly at times coloring the material as it passes through my subconscious. Yet I am constantly astonished by the wide-ranging knowledge the Guides manifest through my typewriter and by their accuracy when a detail is given that can be cross-checked. For instance, I was puzzled by the Guides' account of the adultery committed by Mary, the sister of Lazarus, until I learned that they are not unique in this assertion. Edgar Cayce while in trance also declared that Jesus rescued two adulterous Marys, one of whom was a sister of Lazarus.

Another bit of information intrigued me. The Guides wrote that in a journey by foot which Jesus made from Lazarus' home in Bethany across the Kedron Valley to Jerusalem, He entered the city "through the shepherd's gate." On reading this passage, I saw a chance to check the Guides by determining if this was the logical gate for Jesus to have used. But I did not remember seeing a gate by that name while in the Holy Land ten years ago, and

I could find no such gate listed on my available maps of Jerusalem. Finally, in H. V. Morton's *In the Steps of St. Paul* I read that the entrance which in Christian times is known as St. Stephen's Gate was in Jesus' day called Sheep Gate, and that it is the only one which gives direct access to the Kedron Valley and Bethany.

That is not the only time the Guides have demonstrated their accuracy. For instance: Lisa Chickering and Jeanne Porterfield are internationally known lecturers who exhibit travel films they have made in foreign countries. I met them for the first and only time when they came to Cuernavaca for a day in 1972 to film a segment of *Winter in Mexico*, and shortly after their return to New York City they wrote that Jeanne's mother, Virginia Hobart, had passed on. Sometime later Mrs. Hobart interrupted one of my morning sessions with the Guides to bring a message for Jeanne and Lisa, which I forwarded to them.

On December 27, 1972, Lisa wrote an enthusiastic letter saying that Mrs. Hobart's manner of phrasing her sentences in the message was "almost 100% accurate." She continued, "Her saying, 'God go with you' was always what she said, although she said it in Spanish. She would always say that she would be with us and work for our protection (just as she said in the message) and she always ended her letters to Jeanne with 'my love and devotion to Lisa.' All these things she said to you." Lisa noticed only one or two seeming discrepancies. She said Mrs. Hobart used to sign her letters Mama rather than Mother, and she called her daughter Jeannie rather than little Jeanne, as she did on my typewriter. But Liza noted that the message had been siphoned both through Lily and my subconscious, "and Jeannie of course means little Jeanne." She added, "We do believe the message was from her, as too many unusual ways of speaking such as 'God go with you,' 'working for our protection,' etc. are her ways. Also, in speaking or writing she would break a phrase with 'dear,' as she did throughout your message. An example is, 'I was so happy to hear, dear, that you. . .' and this form was also used in her message sent through you."

Since I had never known Mrs. Hobart and knew nothing of her habits of speech or writing, this would seem to indicate that the message made possible through Lily and the Guides was authentic. But a more dramatic example of their prowess concerns Hale Boggs, the late Majority Leader of the House.

In the fall of 1972, shortly after Hale's disappearance in an airplane while in Alaska, Lindy Boggs telephoned me from Washington to ask if my Guides could indicate where her husband's plane went down, in order to facilitate the rescue mission. At that time U.S. government planes were criss-crossing Alaska daily, from sunup to sundown, in a desperate attempt to find the downed plane while there was still hope of survivors. Lindy said she felt positive that Hale had survived the crash and that several outstanding psychics who volunteered their services assured her that they were "picking up his heartbeat."

The next morning at our regular session, the Guides wrote that the pilot "while trying to skirt a sudden storm which was buffeting the light plane, and seeking to find a way around it, went off course, and the tempest swept the plane in a swirling downdraft into the sea." They said Hale died instantly and painlessly, and that he and the other passengers in the plane were "now sleeping on our side" in the phase beyond death. A few mornings later they again reported on the crash that killed Boggs, declaring: "His wife Lindy will run for his vacated seat and will win. No problem in being elected, and she will be a very good legislator who will perhaps generate great interest in politics for other women, because of her capability and energy. She will go far in this world, and Hale will be able to influence her and her work when he awakens, but only if she desires it from him.

I reported these messages to Lindy, who at that time had no thought of running for Congress and was fervently hoping that Hale had somehow survived the crash. Yet, early in the new year Hale Boggs was officially declared dead and his Congressional seat vacated. Lindy Boggs subsequently ran for that seat in a special election, was handily elected, and became the first woman ever sent to Congress from Louisiana. Somehow the Guides had known it all along.

It is scarcely necessary to remind readers of *A World Beyond* that in the early spring of 1971, when President Nixon had dropped to a new low in public-opinion polls and the betting odds favored the dropping of Vice President Agnew from the Republican ticket, the Guides calmly asserted that the ticket of Nixon and Agnew would win reelection "by a landslide." That is exactly what happened—more than a year and a half later. While making that prediction from the spirit world, Ford also declared that there would be "an overthrow in Chile before too long, and Communists no longer in power." He further asserted that East and West Germany would soon be "somewhat closer together but not totally merged." These also came to pass within the space of two years.

In the same book Arthur Ford wrote that he was not going to tie himself to long-term projects, to avoid becoming earthbound, and I therefore assumed that after completion of that material our mysterious "correspondence" would cease. However, *time* as we regard it here has no meaning on the other side, and the Guides have stated that even a long lifetime in physical body is "as a flash of lightning" in duration when viewed from there.

At any rate, Arthur continues to make himself known each morning through my typewriter, and I have no wish to discourage him. To paraphrase a popular song, I've grown accustomed to his ways. Although Arthur does not figure as prominently in some of the incarnations recounted in this book as in others, it is well to remember that he is helping to dictate *all* of the material. When I refer to "the Guides," it means "Lily, Arthur, and the Group." This, then, is our collaboration.

BOOK ONE

The Palestinian Incarnation

CHAPTER

I

The Holy Family

On a warm, sun-splattered morning in early February our routine was returning to normal. The house-guests from New York had departed, and as I strolled toward the study to begin my daily meditation, I was mentally reviewing the day's schedule: an executive board meeting of the Episcopal Guild, an interview with a prospective cook, and luncheon with friends.

I noted with a sigh the large accumulation of mail that awaited my attention, and after seating myself at the typewriter, I realized that I had not even had time to read what the Guides had written for several days. Thus I had no idea of their current subject matter. Closing my eyes, I tried to still my racing mind; and after a period of quiet meditation I placed my fingers in touch-typing position on the keys, said my usual prayer for protection, and awaited their response.

For the next ten to fifteen minutes there was only the hum of my electric typewriter and the sound of the keys striking the paper. When all activity ceased, I opened my eyes and began scanning the message for the day. To my astonishment, I read as follows:

Let us begin with the birth of a child called Jesus. It was in Bethlehem of Judea at the time of the tax ingathering, and since the story is well known we will say only that as a little girl of seven you saw the bright star and the shepherds who assembled in the village square, and when you heard reports that the star heralded the birth of a babe in Bethlehem, your excitement knew no bounds.

When the twelfth day came for the anointing and cleansing of the babe, you begged to follow the throng to a pool where this was to be done. Your father, Jeremiah, since he was a friend of Joseph's and you were such an eager, bright-eyed little girl, reluctantly took you along, holding your hand tightly so that you would not stray into the thick of the crowd. The event was forever implanted in your soul memory, for a few days earlier when the baby was circumcised, a door was opened and through it you glimpsed a shining aura around the head of this special child. Others thought it was imagination, for you had a vivid one in those days, but always you remembered the shining light encircling the head of the baby Jesus.

Came the wise men, or astrologers, and you gloried to see their rich costumes and foreign appearance. Soon they departed, and then came the warning that Herod would kill all male children under two years of age who had been born in Bethlehem. Because Joseph and Arthur Ford (who was then your father, Jeremiah) had sons nearly the same age named Jesus and Lazarus, they determined to set forth secretly in the night for Egypt. Otherwise they would have been pursued anywhere in Judea or Galilee and their sons stricken down.

Thus, at the tender age of seven you traveled across the desert and waters to Heliopolis, where at last your family gathered with other relatives and friends beside the Nile. The long trek was finished, and for the next several years you studied with a wise group of ex-patriots who themselves had learned many of the secrets of the ancient Egyptians, some of whose ancestors had come from Atlantis. This is all for now.

A thrill of excitement engulfed me as I read these words. Quickly pulling out a desk drawer to retrieve yesterday's dictation from the Guides, I then learned of their promise to divulge the story of Lazarus' alleged sister, Ruth. I could scarcely wait for the next day's session, and twenty-four hours later they resumed the story exactly where they had left off, writing:

The family of Arthur Ford (then Jeremiah) settled down in and around Heliopolis and in the same area, the family of Joseph. You and your younger sister Martha helped tend the little boys, Jesus and Lazarus, who grew strong romping around the fig and olive trees in the desert air. Gathered together in that area of Egypt were scholars from many lands who spoke in several tongues, but Aramaic was familiar to all who had traveled the great trade routes which cut through Galilee. Thus there was talk of excellent quality, and instruction for the children who played at the feet of their elders.

You were ever an apt pupil, as was Lazarus, and when Jesus began to absorb added meaning from the seemingly prosaic instruction, he passed on its occult qualities to you children. Soon, although so young in years, he was the acknowledged leader among you, and for some years until you were into your early teens you continued to live in Heliopolis, with Arthur (Jeremiah) attending to his rabbinical duties and teaching Hebrew, while Joseph created beauty out of fallen timber, working with his tools. Do you remember the master teacher Shinto? He taught you Greek. Did you remember Barraba? He walked with you and held your hand. And what of Maccabee? He loved you then.

The day's writing ended there, and before starting the next session I asked for more information about my "father" Arthur Ford, who was then called Jeremiah. The Guides wrote:

He had been born in Bethlehem of the line of David and was a rabbi and scholar of some repute. He was strict in his beliefs, but warmhearted and loving with children and was delighted with the boy Jesus, who tested his precepts and ideas even as a blue-eyed little lad. Jeremiah studied with Egyptian scholars while in Heliopolis and there became acquainted with the theories about Atlantis (the lost continent) and other mystical lore, including the secrets built into the great pyramid of Cheops. Some of this information he discussed with Ruth, for she was his favorite of the children and the only one of sufficient years, in that Egyptian period, to comprehend what he was saying. She and Lazarus were, as we said, intelligent, quick-witted youngsters, whereas Martha was more slow of speech and thought, and Mary, who was born during the Egyptian sojourn, was still a baby.

Jesus, although just a youngster, was also instructed in these mysteries of the pyramids and the occult, for his father, Joseph, doted on the boy; and realizing that he was unique in his wisdom and understanding for a child of such tender years, Joseph opened doors for him into a world few children could have entered. His mother, Mary, having studied in a temple in Palestine as a small child, instructed Jesus in all that she knew, and the child rapidly developed a mind which in many ways surpassed that of his elders.

The next day Arthur Ford took over the dictation, writing in first person:

When the time came to return to the land of our forefathers, we gathered together many of the ex-patriots who had left because of Herod, and determined to travel together through the desert wastes until we reached Judea, then to go our separate ways. It was a fearsome journey, for the children wept and grew tired. Some could ride on donkeys, but the remainder of us walked, and because you were now in your teens the journey seemed more wearing than when you were an adventuresome child. By the time we reached the Red Sea (that arm of it now known as the Gulf of Suez), all were in a state of exhaustion, but boats took us across the waters, and from then on we drew our second wind for the homeward journey.

On returning to Judea, the separation of families occurred. Jesus and Lazarus, constant companions throughout their early years, wept bitterly as they parted, my family to go to Bethany and the family of Joseph to Nazareth, where his home had previously been. By now Jesus had a young brother and sister, and we of course had added Mary to our brood. Joseph and Mary brought the boy Jesus to Jerusalem on such special occasions as the passover feast, where he would talk with elders of the temple, and once Jesus remained there for several months, that he might study with a priest called Zacharias. Lazarus wished to be with his boyhood chum, so I indulged his pleading and took him also to the temple to study with priests at the same time. But the mind of Jesus outraced his to such an extent that Jesus studied as an adult, while Lazarus took instruction simply as a precocious boy.

Before commencing the next session, I had a question to ask. Reading of Jesus discussing with the elders in the temple brought to mind Arthur Ford's description in A World Beyond *of an exalted school in the next stage of life called "The Temple of Wisdom," I asked if Jesus had ever been associated with it. "Aye,"* *he replied, "as an instructor of highly evolved souls. Yet please try to comprehend," he continued, "that he is not there as a teacher giving daily lessons or sermons, but as a guiding force, an embodiment of perfect harmony. We do not see Jesus in the sense that you see a friend, for it is his presence which is all-pervading. It's impossible to make you understand this, although a few souls in flesh who have had visions of Jesus would know what we mean by the all-pervading presence. Some of them say they have seen him with their outer eyes. We are not able to verify that, since here we neither see nor hear in the sense that you understand the words. God the Father is the* Everything *of which each of us and every creation is a part. Jesus the son is the humanizing element of that* ALL. *The Christ Spirit is the Godpart, for Jesus was a man who lived so perfectly that God sent Son-ship to him with the Christ Spirit."*

I next asked about Arthur Ford's wife in the Palestinian incarnation, and he continued the narrative:

Your mother was a sturdy, honest woman with great powers of recuperation, but she lived for only a short time after we established residency in our new abode just beyond the Mount of Olives. I was a rabbi of the synagogue in Bethany, and after my wife, Sarah, died of the fevers, I turned more and more to you for companionship when the evenings were free. Lazarus spent much of his time at the rabbinical school, and although he showed little aptitude for the priesthood, he nevertheless enjoyed the instruction which honed his sharp, young mind.

Jesus during some of these years studied at a center near the Dead Sea that was operated by occultists known as Hermites or Essenes, for his mind had swiftly outraced the rabbis in Nazareth; and his interest in occult matters, awakened while in Egypt, turned his interest toward the mysteries. He had a cousin John who was living and studying at that place since the death of his elderly parents, and for this reason Joseph permitted his eldest son to live so far from home. The monastery was only a half day's journey from our abode in Bethany, so Lazarus also studied there for part of that time. But since he was my only son, I tried to keep him close at hand to learn his duties as brother, son, and future household head. We had considerable property for those days, for my father had been a cultivator of the soil and had bequeathed me several holdings. These Lazarus would learn to manage while also pursuing his Biblical studies.

Joseph, too, was rather affluent for the times, owning

by then several houses he had built, and a spacious woodworking shop in busy Nazareth that a kinsman had watched
over for him during the Holy Family's years of self-exile
in Egypt.

After the death of my wife, Sarah, you took over as
mother of my brood until the time came that Jonathan,
the son of a neighboring family called Asher-ben, took
you to be his wife. He was older than you by two decades,
and because of his business interests he moved to Jericho,
so that we grieved at your departure. But Martha was
turning into a good little housekeeper; and Mary, when
she was not dreaming by the brook, assisted with the household. Lazarus was a bookish boy who also dreamed and
read, and so devoted was he to his friend Jesus that
whenever the Passover brought the family of Joseph to
Jerusalem, the two lads were inseparable.

*Fascinated to read of this boyhood fellowship between Jesus
and Lazarus, I asked at a subsequent session whether the two
had known each other in a previous incarnation, and the Guides
wrote: "Of course. They had been brothers in a previous lifetime
in ancient Egypt when both were adepts of the mysteries and
also in Old Testament days. But we do not wish to go into that
here, because they were not known to you then." Arthur Ford
then returned to the narrative, addressing me directly:*

From time to time you visited us after your marriage,
and each time it was a new wrench when you departed,
for although you now had a child of your own, the motherli-
ness you had bestowed on my other three youngsters had
cemented a bond that would not be broken, then or evermore. The years passed. Lazarus grew to manhood and
became a scholar of repute. You were lonely in Jericho,
despite your busy life as the wife of a successful
businessman. Thus, one day as you trudged along the
desert area around the Dead Sea, seeking solace and

remembering the long years of exile in Egypt when you were a carefree child, you came to an abrupt decision. There was one whom you had always followed even as a child, when he was so much younger. The boy Jesus. Now he was a man and beginning to stir interest in the area of Galilee, as you had heard from Lazarus. You would seek him out and join the little band who recognized his superiority and his supreme message.

On bended knee you asked Jonathan for permission to go to Galilee, but when he learned why you sought permission he was angered, saying that the man Jesus talked nonsense and was going against the teachings of the synagogue. He therefore forbade you to join Jesus and his followers, and you were deeply disheartened, for something within you kept whispering that this was the truth and the light.

By now you had two children, one still a toddler, and although you dearly loved them, they failed to fill the void in your life—the need for something above self and self-seeking. Thus, when you later heard that Jesus was preaching near the Dead Sea (for word spread like wildfire in those days before electrical communication), you cast fear aside and sped into the desert, running on the wings of the song in your heart, until at a distance across the burning sands, but sheltered beneath a small grove of trees, you glimpsed the friend of your childhood surrounded by many people.

The day's writing stopped there, and after reading what Arthur had written, I again seemed to be reliving that dramatic time under hypnosis when I had rushed into the desert to hear Jesus. Since the method Jane Winthrop uses is a light form of hypnosis the subject seems to be operating on two levels at once: aware of the present-day room and the hypnotist, but living occurrences of the past. I smile to recall that as I glimpsed Jesus in the distance,

I exclaimed, "There he is! Oh, there he is, surrounded by a multitude *of people." And when Jane asked how many were in the crowd, I said excitedly, "Oh, it's a multitude! There must be at least a hundred people." In her dry, droll way she responded, "I've always wondered how big a multitude was."*

I was now impatient to learn more about the incident from the Guides, and they began the next session as if there had been no interruption, writing:

Joining the outskirts of the crowd, you lifted yourself soul and spirit to the words of this man who spoke with such lyricism that the very birds seemed to halt their songs to heed his words. "Wilt thou be seeker and servant?" he asked. "Then follow me, for we are all servants of our Father in heaven who blew life into our forms and gave us each a piece of His own Being. For God is *ALL*. Seek and ye shall find, knock and it will be opened unto you, for as surely as we seek Him Who gave us being, so will He seek us out at every moment and heed our prayers and supplications. He nurtures us as a mother her helpless infant. . . ." And at that a pang of conscience smote you, Ruth, for had you not rushed away with scarcely a backward glance at your two youngsters?

Jesus, reading your troubled mind, smiled at you through the throng of people and spake, "Fear not, for as an earthly father goes forth to provide food for his family, so our Father will watch over your little ones and keep them safe from harm, for you are hungry for that which your husband and uncles are unable to provide. You who hunger after the word of God follow me, and we shall seek the path that leads to eternal salvation."

At this you brightened, and when the crowd had begun to disperse, you knelt before your childhood friend, saying, "Lord, Lord, for I know that you are He; ever hath you guided me even with the mouth of a babe. Permit me, O Lord, to follow thee."

But Jesus spake, saying, "Have thought to the pledge

you gave before God to follow thy husband, and remember the children who depend on thee for a mother's loving care. Return thou to thy husband and the household of thy making; but when I am in this area, I shall see thee again. Meanwhile, remember the words of Him who gave us life: 'Thou art my beloved children. Feast on me.' "

Filled to overflowing with joyousness and love, you returned to your family. But your husband, Jonathan, flamed with anger on learning where you had been, having defied his command, and would have none of you. You were put into a room and guarded by servants, so that liberty was removed from you. When at last you gained release from solitude, you tried to be meek and submissive, but it was not in the nature of Ruth, then or ever, to be guided by another's will.

Would the Guides never cease to chastise me? At the start of the next session I asked, "Why did Ruth always resent having others impose their will on her?" Their reply: "Not always, my dear, but too often for comfort. In the beginning of Creation she resisted evil and temptation, but gradually came to feel superior to those who had not done so. As this soul memory was brought into flesh again and again, she developed a sense of superiority that still needs to be overcome. Not a bad person, remember, but a rather willful one who needs to cultivate humility above all other traits and to glorify the accomplishments of others rather than self." This admonition was disconcerting, since numerous people have commented on my "humbleness," but I am the first to admit that the Guides seem to know me better than I know myself. Referring to the confinement in Jericho, they then continued:

When the opportunity for escape presented itself, you took with you your smallest daughter and started on foot toward the house of Lazarus. But the child cried out with the torment of the desert and lack of sufficient water, so you returned her to her father's home. Then, after a few days of rest, you slipped forth alone and at last arrived exhausted at Lazarus' house in Bethany. Martha greeted you warmly, but sobbingly told you that Mary was missing from the home.

You later learned that Mary had followed Jesus into the desert, even as you had done, and when Mary found him alone in meditation she threw herself at his feet, telling him of her love for him and begging to be permitted to serve him in any way. Jesus talked with her as man to woman, telling her of his love for her, but explaining as gently as possible that it was his mission to love all men, all women, all children—sinners and publicans, the rich and the poor, the humble and the mighty—for only thus would he be able to explain God's rule of love to all mankind. She wept bitterly, yearning for his love to shine more purely and fiercely on her than on others. But when at last she understood that he was not hers alone, but a part of every man and woman on the face of the earth, she quieted and listened while he spake to her such words of wisdom as she had never known.

"Love one another, Mary my beloved," he told her. "Each is a part of our Creator, and thus we serve best our Lord God when we serve those who are nearer to us than hands and feet. Hold thyself in readiness to be His handmaiden at all times, and through example show to others that they too are dearly beloved of God. Treasure thy chastity as an offering to our Creator, and if the time ever dawns that thou findest a man worthy of thy exclusiveness, then take him as thy wedded spouse. Until that day, hold thyself in readiness for Him who asks us to pray: Our Father Who art in heaven, hallowed be Thy name, Thy kingdom come, Thy will be done on earth and through me as it is in heaven. Give us this day our needed bread, and forgive those who trespass against us even as we forgive those who do aught to us; for Thine is the kingdom and I am Thy creation, and all will find solace in Thy loving care, Amen."

Mary treasured the prayer, and deep within her heart knew that she was unworthy to have yearned to become the spouse of such as Jesus, whom she had loved from her cradle. Reluctantly she returned to the house of Lazarus and awaited Jesus' coming, for he had promised to see her there in a few suns.

There had been no mention of Arthur Ford, my "father" called Jeremiah, for sometime, so I asked what he had been doing while Ruth was held captive by her husband and whether he knew that Mary was in love with her childhood playmate, Jesus. Arthur then took over the typewriter, with these words: "At that time I was no longer in the flesh, having passed on before Jesus began his preaching. You wonder about my death. It was not an untimely one, for in those days the soul dwelt less long in the body than in ancient Biblical times. I was all of fifty-seven when the time came for me to make the crossover, and although an injury hastened the withdrawal, it was as if the time had come for me to depart, leaving my affairs in good order.

"Thus, what seemed a minor sickness suddenly developed a burning temperature, and when it struck my heart I passed quickly, with no time even to say good-bye to you, my daughter, for you had not realized the terminal nature of my illness and were at home with your family in Jericho. Well, by then Lazarus was nearly a full-grown man and his friend Jesus was at that time in Nazareth, helping with his father's business."

Sometime later recalling that in A World Beyond *Arthur declared that as Jeremiah he had a number of children, some younger and some older than Ruth, I asked why he now spoke of Ruth as the eldest. It was Lily who replied, "Arthur had an earlier family, for he was much older than your mother, and the children by the first marriage were so nearly grown that they did not need to make the long trek to Egypt." There was no further elaboration.*

CHAPTER

2

The Hidden Years

*For me, the narrative was moving
along too rapidly. It was interesting to reflect on the possibility
that I had once walked the earth in Biblical days, but I was far
more intrigued by the opportunity to learn additional facts about
the boyhood of Jesus, of which the New Testament provides such
a paucity of material. I therefore asked, as meekly as possible, if
the Guides would interrupt the flow of their story to go back
and supply more details of those "missing years," and they wrote:*

To return to the boyhood of Jesus. He was an uncom-
monly handsome boy of sturdy build, with deep blue eyes,
and blond or light brown hair. Leaving Egypt at an early
age, when none other so young could have grasped the
full meaning of the Egyptian mysteries, he bade good-bye
to Lazarus in Judea. Then his parents took him and his
younger brother and sister to Nazareth, where his father
resumed his woodworking business, and they settled down
in the small house above a cave that Joseph had hand-built
for his bride, Mary, some years before. The neighbors
welcomed them with mixed emotions, having heard
rumors of the strange happenings at the time of the birth
of this extraordinary child, and of those who came to pay
homage when a star hung over the cave where he was
born in Bethlehem.

Some muttered that it was fanciful thinking, but others
were disturbed at the possibility that the prophecies had

been fulfilled in this little boy. King of the Jews? Impossible! Yet was there not something in the prophecies about the line of David, a birth in Bethlehem, and a man coming out of Nazareth? Why else, some reasoned, would Joseph have had to flee to Egypt with this child, to escape the wrath of Herod? Some even recalled rumors that Mary had been big with child before she married her betrothed, and it was indeed strange by Mosaic law for Joseph to take unto himself a wife who was already heavy with child.

Reading these words, I became curious about how Jesus happened to be born to Mary and Joseph, rather than to some other couple. Arthur Ford, in the earlier material that he dictated for A World Beyond, *discoursed at length about the "heavenly computer" which souls in the spirit world employ before returning to flesh as the child of a particular mother. Ford had also emphasized that we can earn the right to select our own parents and the circumstances into which we are born. I therefore asked the Guides, "Why was Jesus born in particular to Mary, with Joseph as his foster father?" They replied: "Jesus and Mary had been together since the beginning of time, the closest affinity that two souls are ever able to achieve. So like unto each other that it is like two eyes seeing the same object simultaneously in one head. Joseph was ever with them throughout the passage of time, but this is beside the point in the account that we are giving you, for you were not then with them. They were exalted souls, all three, ever accustomed to abiding by God's will in all matters, and subjecting* Self *to* Higher Command. *They are souls who did not originally stray from the Creator when released as sparks from His glorious Being."*

The latter was obviously a reference to the explanation of man's creation that Lily had recounted in A Search for the Truth. *"The entities that became all of us were once segments of His Glorious Self," Lily had written through my typewriter a decade earlier, "and as each radiated off from Him it became a little breath, with a chance to grow and develop into a real and significant unit that could shine in God's true grace. These little entities set boldly along the path that would lead back to their Maker, but along the way the temptations proved too strong for most of them. Because the Son of God was able to reject those temptations, He is able to return to the earth again and again, without any of its hampering limitations of time and space and body." This reference would also explain what the Guides meant (in Chapter 1) when they said that in the beginning of Creation Ruth had successfully resisted evil and temptation, but that her downfall began when she started to feel superior to those other souls who had not done so.*

After meditating on these solemn thoughts for a time, I placed my fingertips on the typing keys, and the narrative resumed:

Because Joseph and Mary behaved in a normal manner, not putting on airs but going about their daily tasks like any other married couple with children, the rumors were soon laid to rest and they were accepted in the community. Jesus helped his father in the woodworking shop and also attended classes taught by the rabbis of Nazareth, until in his twelfth year he stayed behind in Jerusalem after his parents took him there for the Passover.

Mary and Joseph, as we all read in the New Testament, were heavy of heart when they discovered Jesus missing from the large caravan that had begun its journey to the north, and returning immediately to Jerusalem, which was only a half day's journey, they located him in the temple, where he was baffling the elders with his erudition and profundity. "How is it," the elders asked the distrait parents, "that this lad of tender years speaks as a prophet, fully conversant with the text of our laws and prophecies, yet understanding inner meanings as well?

The relieved parents showed no embarrassment at the question, and it was Joseph who replied, "Our son has gifts that we do not comprehend and knowledge that is beyond our ken, but who knows the wondrous ways of our Lord God of Israel?"

The elders urged that the boy be left in their care, saying that someday he might even rise as high as membership in the Sanhedrin, but the wrench was too much for Mary at that time. The parents agreed to consider the proposal, and after returning with Jesus to Nazareth, they discussed it at length, finally leaving the decision to the boy Jesus, who said it was time that he should be about his Father's business. And they understood that by father he meant the God of Israel. Thus they prepared his meager stock of clothing, and when next a caravan was going to Jerusalem, they permitted their son to travel with it, but not without tears on the part of his mother and admonitions from his heavy-hearted father.

The boy flourished in the intellectual atmosphere of the Temple Most High in Jerusalem, and within a few months had grasped all that they could teach him. His parents suffered acutely from his absence, and before long Joseph went to Jerusalem to ask if the boy were ready to return home. Jesus readily agreed, for he missed his parents and the little ones; and because he was wise beyond his tender years, he knew that there was little more the elders were able to teach him.

After the writing ceased and I read this segment, I felt that I understood its meaning. Highly evolved souls who have made the most of their previous earthly embodiments obviously have an advantage over those who have frittered away opportunities. Edgar Cayce while in trance declared that Jesus had had thirty incarnations, although he identified only eight of them, beginning with Amilius and Adam. Presumably this would explain the Master's enigmatic statement that "before Abraham was, I am."

Returning to the narrative of Jesus' childhood, the Guides wrote:

Thus Jesus went home to Nazareth again to work in his father's shop, and for a time Lazarus visited him there, having returned with Joseph and Jesus to Nazareth. Then came word that the son of Elizabeth and Zacharias, who were now dead, was studying with the Essenes at Qumran beside the Dead Sea, and because Jesus within himself felt that there he would be taught more of the mysteries, he requested leave of his parents to be permitted to join John for a time.

Jeremiah (Arthur Ford) had come for his son, to return him to Bethany, and because Lazarus also pleaded to be permitted to accompany Jesus to the Qumran monastery, Mary and Joseph agreed that Jeremiah would take both boys to the monastery and inspect it to see if they would be permitted to remain for a time. The two lads and Jeremiah made the trip in less than three days, sleeping under the stars by night, and when they saw the monastery in the hills above the Dead Sea, both lads fell in love with it. Jesus had a warm reunion with his cousin John, whom he had not seen since two Passovers ago in Jerusalem, and Jeremiah gave permission for them to stay awhile, although Lazarus was to return home within sixty days. Jesus remained for two more months beyond Lazarus' departure. Then Joseph came for him, and John accompanied them back to Nazareth for a time, before returning to the monastery.

At the next Passover the family of Mary and Joseph did not go, as was their custom, to Jerusalem, because Joseph was ailing and none seemed to know the cause of it. The weakness had come upon him, and though he continued to struggle at his workbench, the perspiration would pour from him and the weakness would force him to a couch. Jesus, concerned for the beloved man who had been more than a father to him in the years since his birth, anguished over him, sponging his face and trying to double his own work to spare Joseph, but the condition worsened. The power of God had not yet entered the body of the lad, and he was thus unaware of the enormous healing powers that would one day be his. At this time all he could do for Joseph was pray and treat him with tender solicitude.

Several months later, while editing this material for publication, I asked whether Jesus at this particular time had any intimation of his ultimate destiny. Their response was: "The boy Jesus knew within self that he was different from others. He felt an inner guidance so strong that he would not have thought to go against that guidance. Yet the curtain had not yet been lifted on his mission, and for the time being he had no special healing powers. That would come when the Christ Spirit descended upon him at the time of his baptism by John."

At this later period I also learned that Edgar Cayce had once been asked when the knowledge came to Jesus that he was to be the savior of the world. The entranced Cayce replied, "When he fell, in Eden." This was, of course, a reference to his alleged earlier incarnation as Adam, but we do not automatically bring back with us all memories of previous earth lives. At the next session the Guides returned to the subject of Joseph's illness, writing:

Mary's last child was on the way, and it was thus a busy household. Joseph, sensing that his time was near, spent as much time as possible with his beloved wife and children, but one day he closeted himself with Jesus to tell him the strange happenings concerning his birth and the messages from angels both to himself and the beautiful young Mary before they were wed.

"Never fail to believe, son, that as Mary is thy mother, so is our God of Israel thy father, for thou wert born in a most strange and holy manner, with a strange light about thy fair head even as I assisted thee from thy mother's womb."

It was the first time Jesus had been told of his miraculous

conception, but instead of surprise he expressed only appreciation that his father had found words to tell him of it. "Father Joseph," he said, "although I have not heard the story until now from human lips, our Father has shown it to me in dreams and visions, so that although I knew that I am not flesh of thy flesh and blood of thy blood, thou art dearer to me than anyone in flesh except my beloved mother. I revere thee above all men and pray for thy recovery."

Joseph, filled with emotion at those sweet and loving words, said, "Son, fear not if I go on to our fathers, for thou art now nearly a man, and God's ways are not our ways. Watch over thy mother and our little flock, for if I am called, they could have no better shepherd than thee."

That night Joseph slept away, lying beside his beloved Mary, and her anxious heart knew the moment that his great heart stopped its beating. Thus Jesus became the head of the household of Joseph, and he spent much time instructing his younger brother in how best to carry on the business before he would begin his Father's work. Such complete understanding was there between mother and son that Mary raised no protest when he at last bade fond farewell.

For a number of years thereafter Jesus traveled widely to learn at the feet of other masters. During those wandering years he sat in the temples of the most high, conferring with holy men and exchanging views with them about the substance of life and the glory of God.

At the beginning of the next session, in response to my mental question, the Guides wrote: "You ask where Jesus traveled in some of those unrecorded Biblical years. As we have said, he stayed longer in Egypt than Biblical scholars have assumed, having reached the age of seven when the return trek with his family to Nazareth began. After the death of Joseph, Jesus made a journey through the Fertile Crescent and far beyond, to study with monks and masters in Persia and India. He returned also to Egypt for a time, and in all these sacred places he was initiated into the secret teachings. Except for their influence on the mind and heart of Jesus they need no telling here; but influence him they did, and help to shape the character of his ministry."

My curiosity was by no means satisfied. Rather, it was doubly piqued by the reference to "secret teachings," and at a later time I asked the Guides if they would comment further on this matter. They replied: "The initiation Jesus underwent at Brotherhood gatherings in Egypt, Persia, India, and elsewhere dealt with the understanding of universal laws as they pertain to physical matter, and the means of disassembling ions and atoms so that they can be reassembled on the other side of a wall or barrier. Understanding of the law of harmony in music and color. How to heal and what to to about those who would not believe without seeing with their physical eyes. The fine art of meditation and the science of knowing another's innermost thoughts. This knowledge is preserved even today in remote areas of the Far and Middle East, and the secrets are so guarded that none may penetrate this innermost wisdom unless he is an adept who has developed a thorough understanding of it in previous lives. Thus, this glimmer of truth will be preserved until mankind has progressed sufficiently to be able to handle the mysteries without endangering the truth and harming others. Advanced souls are already beginning to spread some awareness of these secret teachings, and as the Aquarian Age progresses, more will be divulged." With that, I had to be content. And now, to return to the narrative:

When at last Jesus was ready to begin his teachings, it was natural that he should return to the area of his childhood where his mother still lived. But the fact that he was considered a native son worked against rather than for him, inasmuch as this has ever been the way with those who excel in philosophy and dreams.

"Is that not the son of Joseph the carpenter?" was heard throughout Nazareth; and because they considered him a pretender, they drove him from the synagogue, for they thought he was blaspheming those who for centuries had conducted their services in the rigid way of the prophets. Thus he departed thence.

Setting forth once again from his mother's house, Jesus went straightaway to the River Jordan and walked southward. Seeing afar off a man dressed wildly, with shaggy beard and hair, he approached the group to whom the man was preaching. It was a long time since he had seen his cousin, but when John offered baptism to all who would dedicate their lives to God, Jesus stepped forward, whereupon John, who recognized his cousin, was glad. After his baptism the dove lit on Jesus' shoulder and a shaft of light broke through the heavens, encircling his body. Then a great knowing came to John, so that he said, "He it is who fulfills the testament. He it is for whom the world waiteth, and blessed is he who looks on him."

And Jesus, upon whom the spirit of truth and the Christ consciousness descended at that moment, recognized Elias in John. Thus were the teachings of the prophets fulfilled.

Reading what the Guides had written about the baptismal scene, I felt a tingle of excitement, as if all of us had been witnesses to that hallowed event. The Guides had earlier said this was the moment when Jesus the man became Jesus the Christ. Now they were saying that also at this time Jesus knew his beloved cousin John to be the reincarnation of Elias, who had returned to herald the coming of Christ. That Jesus possessed such knowledge was demonstrated in the latter days of his ministry, when the disciples questioned him about the Old Testament prophecy (see the Foreword), and Jesus identified the beheaded John the Baptist as Elias.

The next day the writing continued:

Jesus tarried for a time to talk with John, and so many came to Jesus offering to follow him that, fearing personal elation, he went into the wilderness to pray that he might overcome all temptation and to thank God for his Son-ship. Within self he struggled with the earthly temptations of power and lust, the leaving of his beloved family to become God's chosen instrument, and all other temptings. After forty days he had downed them all, never again to be tempted through physical means, and when he had made his peace within self he went straightaway to Capernaum.

One morning while walking along the shores of Galilee he saw two fishermen mending their nets. Suddenly within himself he knew that these were men whom God wished to work with him, and to them he said, "Cast down thy nets and follow me."

The sunburned, rugged men looked up in surprise, and Andrew said, "What wishest thou with us?"

Again the inner prompting, and Jesus replied, "Come with me and I will make thee fishers of men."

Simon (later Peter), puzzling the meaning of the words, said, "What meanest thou that you want to make us fishers of men, for we are fishermen in the Sea of Galilee and are trained to catch fish."

"Yea," Jesus responded, "but others are also trained for that, whereas together we will seek out those who hunger after the Lord's works and will show them the way and the light."

His tone was impelling, and Peter, after a glance at his brother Andrew (who was a follower of the Baptizer named John), said, "Let us go along for a time and see whereof he speaks." The two men arose as one, stepped from the boat, and left it in the care of those others who were hired to assist them.

Straightaway Jesus walked to another nearby boat and there spotted James and John, who were mending nets. To them he said, "Why waitest thou? We are all brothers, and God has beckoned us to follow in His way. Come and follow me."

John, the younger, leaped from the boat and James followed. And they walked with Jesus and the others to the synagogue, where they knelt together and pledged their lives to Him who gave them life.

Impressed by the willingness of these four fishermen to abandon their work so abruptly and follow a stranger, I asked the Guides if Jesus had known them in previous incarnations. The Guides chose to broaden the question by replying: "Jesus had known ALL of the twelve disciples in previous incarnations, and he was instructed by God the Father which ones to choose. Jesus did not entirely agree with some of the choices, but he did not question the vibrations within self when he accosted these various men. Always within self he had been given these signs of what was right or wrong, even as a small boy, and when he tarried behind in the Temple of Jerusalem as a lad, it was the Father speaking within him that caused him to do so.

"The disciples were selected not for their spiritual superiority or mental powers, but in order to represent many different kinds of souls then inhabiting bodies: Fiery temper in Peter, but goodness of soul. Erudition in Andrew, and temporal power in Matthew. Modesty in Philip, and simplicity in Bartholomew. Sweetness in John, and a tender, loving heart. So it goes. Judas was chosen for his opportunity to overcome jealousy and ambition, and was given as much chance as any man to put others on a par with self and withstand temptation. Yet some succeed where others fail. Thus, every type of so-called human nature was represented in these disciples, who had been companions, rivals, friends, relatives, or even enemies of Jesus and each other in previous embodiments."

The Guides then returned to the dramatic episode beside the Sea of Galilee, writing:

After praying together in the synagogue, the four fishermen would have returned to their nets, but Jesus said, "Nay, thou art the first of the apostles and we would go now to Cana, where a wedding feast is being prepared."

"For thee, Rabbi?" asked John. And Jesus replied, "Nay, we are bridegrooms of our Father who is in heaven, but let us hie to Cana, where my work is about to begin."

Thus they hired donkeys and rode up into the hills and arrived late in the day at Cana, where the new disciples met Mary the mother of Jesus and other members of the wedding party. The host greeted them warmly, as if he had been prepared for their coming, but in a little while the wine was gone, and Mary, caressing her son with the look in her blue eyes, said, "Son, it is an embarrassment for him who is our friend and kinsman by marriage."

Jesus sighed a deep sigh, as if dreading the step he was about to take. Then he directed servants to fill the casks with water, and after they had done so he told them to serve it individually to the guests.

"Serve water at a wedding?" one asked in surprise, but Mary directed them to do as her son requested, and when it came from the casks the wine was sweet and full-bodied, so that guests expressed surprise at the excellence of the wine so late in the festivities. Then Jesus and his four disciples said good-bye and returned to Capernaum.

"What manner of man is this," Andrew asked his brother as they drew nigh unto their house in Capernaum, "that water could be made into wine at the speaking of a word?"

"I know not," Simon Peter answered, "but there is a magnetism about him that pulls forth my love, so that I seem only to want his company."

"I too," Andrew said wonderingly, "so let us explain to our father and we will go with him for a time."

James and John had meanwhile reached a similar conclusion. Their love for Jesus flamed brightly, and with his tranquillity and assurance he drew them as moths to a flame. They too puzzled about the wine, and because it was not the best time for fishing, they also accompanied him as he set forth down the River Jordan, where he talked to others along the way. Some there were who needed healing, and when a word from Jesus or a touch of his hand made them well again, the word spread and he was surrounded by throngs who listened intently to his message of love.

During those first days and weeks of his ministry Jesus selected other disciples from among his followers, and when he finally added Matthew and Judas to his band they were complete, for an even dozen was the number that Jesus needed for his plan, and he himself made thirteen. Thus his full-time ministry began.

At a much later date, in scanning the four Gospels for their accounts of this period, I noted disagreement among them as to the manner in which Jesus recruited the apostles. Since none of the chroniclers of the New Testament may have been eyewitnesses to these stirring events, and certainly Lily and Arthur Ford were not, I cannot vouch for the authenticity of the Guides' account. But they claim to have read it in the akashic records, on which all events since the beginning of time are said to be imprinted.

3

The Sisters of Lazarus

For a long time there had been no mention of Ruth, but I was so entranced with the story of Jesus that I failed to notice the omission. Then one morning, after concluding the usual session with the Guides, I read these words:

When the time came for Jesus to begin his full-time ministry, it was as if an unquenchable yearning overwhelmed Ruth, and she pleaded with her husband to go with her to hear his teaching in the desert. But Jonathan was adamant. This was not according to the Torah, he insisted, and because he was a busy, stubborn man he forbade her to join the throngs who surrounded the man she had known as a child. Each day became harder for Ruth to bear, because Lazarus and her two sisters were frequently in the company of Jesus, and often he visited with them on his journeys in and around Jerusalem.

At last, when her husband declared that she was forbidden even to think of it anymore, the ego within her spoke, and she vowed that until she had joined the followers of Jesus she would eat no further and would not sit at the table of her spouse. This was not the first "hunger strike," but it lasted until she was emaciated and without energy. Jonathan secretly viewed her with concern and at last gave permission that for one day she would be permitted to join the followers, although she would have to return home by nightfall. Ruth then fled happily across the desert on foot, not daring to take a donkey, since she had no intention of returning. Near the mouth of the Jordan she glimpsed the assemblage and within the group her sister Martha.

"Sister, sister, what has become of you?" Martha asked with alarm, for Ruth was thin and weak from fasting.

"It is naught now," she replied, "for I am come to hear words for which my soul hungers and to feed myself with soul delight at the banquet of our Lord Jesus." She knelt before the Master, and touching the hem of his robe, pressed her face to it, sighing, "Master, for thee I would gladly surrender the whole world."

Jesus touched her light brown hair, then, bringing her to her feet, said, "Ruth, Ruth, what of thy responsibilities to thy family?"

Her tears flowed as she bowed her head, saying, "Surely, Master, there are better foods than that which is consumed at mealtime, and surely there are better ways of serving our God than through tidying the house and listening to the chatter of children."

"Yea, Ruth," he replied, "there are finer fruits than those which grow on arbor and tree, but as to the latter part of thy saying, serving others is still the better way of serving Him."

Ruth was crestfallen. Surely the world was against her, that everyone wished her at home with her husband and children. She followed Jesus and some of his disciples to the home of her brother Lazarus, where food was being spread on the tables and where Mary draped herself at the feet of Jesus as he spoke to them in parables. Ruth flitted back and forth between the kitchen and sala, straining to hear his words while serving the table and also assisting Martha in the kitchen. Martha was riled with Mary, who chose to sit at the feet of the Master rather than help with the preparations, but Ruth shushed her, saying, "Is it not for that that we were born, to learn of our God from him who came directly from God in order to instruct us? It is true that the followers need meat and drink, and that it is our lot to serve man, but surely Mary has chosen the better part to be at his feet."

Martha looked at her older sister Ruth and shrewdly guessed what was in her heart. "It is because he is like unto a son to you that you love him so." And Ruth replied, "Nay, for such a son would I have given the world, but it is that he is like unto the moon and sun, the stars and the earth all rolled into one. Martha, we knew him from babyhood, and never have I known such another. From the moment that he looked directly into my eyes while I held him as a babe I recognized the forces of God. When he began to speak it was not as a toddler speaks in lisps, for he spoke with full and rounded tone, uttering such wisdom as I have never heard even from our sainted father. Oh, that our father had lived unto this day, for often did he and I converse about this wondrous child Jesus, who seemed from babyhood to be an ordained priest of the temple. How our father, Jeremiah, enjoyed his conversations with the boy Jesus, and how proud he was when he addressed elders in the temple, speaking such wisdom as caused chills to run along the spines of the listeners. None spake such words of wisdom since the beginning of time, and if he will not bid me go hence from him, I shall follow him to the end of time."

This was the first mention of Arthur Ford since his death as Jeremiah, and when I asked about it at one of the morning sessions, Arthur assured me that in those times he was as aware of the earthly progress of his family and friends as he is now that he is again in spirit form. Much more so, in fact, since most of those on "the other side" in those times were vitally concerned with the earthly drama of the man who had become the Christ. Then the Guides took over, writing:

Martha, on hearing those words about Jesus from her

elder and more knowledgeable sister, understood the yearnings of Mary, and her heart softened toward her. When the food was on the table, they joined the disciples and Lazarus, and after Jesus had blessed the food, they ate and listened to him speak. It was the happiest day in the life of Ruth, who held to her heart each syllable of his musical voice, and in pondering his meaning she seemed to understand nuances that some of the others failed to grasp.

"Feed my sheep," he said, and while several men said it was not the feeding time, Ruth knew that he was seeking to nourish their souls. "Judge not lest ye also be judged," he said, and Ruth instantly knew that even though her husband had spoken judgment against her by decrying her interest in the Lord Jesus, to judge her husband in return would bring harsh judgment on her at the Day of Judgment.

At this point it was interesting to note that the Palestinian Ruth believed in an actual Day of Judgment, when God would presumably dispatch the good souls to heaven and condemn the evil ones to hell. The Guides have repeatedly stressed in their writings that God judges no man. They declare that each time after leaving physical body we review our past incarnation and serve as our own judge, noting our mistakes and pledging to work to overcome our shortcomings and misdeeds upon returning to flesh.

At the next day's session, the Guides resumed where they had left off, writing:

Ruth intuitively sensed that Mary was overwhelmingly in love with the Jesus whom she had known since earliest babyhood, and although nothing would have pleased her more than for this precious little sister to wed the one whom she adored, something within her declared that this man would never choose among his flock to take a wife.

Rather, he was giving himself to all who would heed his words, without differentiation.

For three days Ruth tarried in the home of her brother, who in so many ways reminded her of their beloved father (Arthur Ford), and during those days she heard from the lips of Jesus enough wisdom to last the world for an eternity. In his gentle but effective way he taught Ruth, sometimes directly and at other times through parables, that it was her mission in this life to return to her family and care for her husband and children. Then, equipped with the new enlightenment Jesus had imparted to her, she could help them also to see the light. When she understood from the Master that she was important to his mission in helping others see the light of the world, beginning at her own fireside, she gladly departed hence to her home in Jericho. And so glad was Jonathan to see her in good health and spirits after her sojourn with Lazarus that he welcomed her to his heart and his bed, and so gentle had he become that she was able to tell him all that had passed while she listened to the son of God.

This intrigued him, for he then understood that Jesus was not preaching against the scriptures, but actually expanding their hidden meaning and revealing facts which hitherto had seemed masked in obscurity. When Jesus came again to the River Jordan, Jonathan therefore accompanied Ruth to meet and hear him, and in a brilliant light he was converted to his teachings and ready to die for the son of God. Happy now, Ruth and Jonathan as a team gathered up their children and handservants to become followers of Jesus, spreading his message and holding services to instruct in the teachings of the Lord.

Levi, in The Aquarian Gospel of Jesus the Christ, *also declared that Ruth eventually converted her husband to Christianity. Thus, before beginning the next day's sessions with the*

*Guides, I asked what Jonathan's karma had been that caused
his earlier stubbornness in accepting the teachings of Jesus. The
Guides replied: "Not so much karmic, as his deep faith in that
which he had been taught from babyhood, so that like some living
today, he accepts only the written word and childhood teachings
as fact. He was hard to convince, but Jonathan underwent a
cleansing experience while listening to Jesus speak, which evangeli-
cal churches today would call 'being saved.' There's no harm
in demanding proof so long as one's mind is sufficiently open
to accept that which awaits all who will heed the voice within."*

*I asked if I now know Jonathan, in my present embodiment,
and they replied enigmatically, "Not to be discussed at this time."
The writing then continued:*

The day following the conversion of Jonathan, the husband of Ruth, the entire group of followers journeyed
up the Jordan toward the Sea of Galilee, and after they
stopped to rest at the home of a kinsman of Lazarus and
Ruth, Jonathan became filled with the spirit of God and
began preaching as eloquently as any man in the land
except the Lord Jesus. This filled Ruth with rapturous
joy, and she afterward knelt at his feet, saying that she
would wash his feet. But he drew her to him, saying, "It
was I who was wrong, and I who should kneel at *thy* feet,
for through you I have sampled the wonders of God's
kingdom. Now I am His humblest of servants, and whither
this man of God sends us, there will we go and abide
with Him."

For some days they tarried in the Galilean area and
gathered unto them many who drew nigh to hear about
the strange conversions performed by the man Jesus, and
of the many miracles he seemed able to perform. Some
had witnessed the miracle of the loaves and fishes, but
they thought it to be a form of magic or sorcery, since
he was only the son of a Nazarene named Joseph, who
was a worker of wood. But when they saw that humble
fishermen and even the once-scorned tax collector,

Matthew, had given up all in the name of Jehovah, whose son was said to walk among them, they began following the disciples and particularly the man Jesus, whom they had previously doubted.

Ruth moved among the throngs, comforting one here and another there, and hearing their petitions to be healed by Jesus. Jonathan too began attending to the suffering, and although no miracles sprang from his touch, he nevertheless effected seeming miracles by giving comfort and loving attention to the ailing.

After dwelling briefly with kinsmen on the outskirts of Tiberius, they went on to Capernaum, which Ruth loved; and she would sit dreamily in the sun at the steps of the tabernacle, gazing across olive groves to the Sea of Galilee, with its busily plying boats, and to the native hills beyond. She occasionally recognized some of those whom she had known as a teenager during the Egyptian sojourn, because Capernaum was on the main trade route between Syria, Persia, and Egypt, and many were the opportunities to speak to them in various tongues that she had learned as a child in Egypt, when they paused for refreshment in this fishing and trading village beside the lake.

Peter came oft to sit beside her and marvel at the wonders wrought in their lives by the master, and at times he would quote olden scriptures to explain how the Son of God came to be among them at this time in the world's history. But it was Andrew who sat thoughtfully beside her and wove a spell over his listeners by telling of the dreams and portents he had experienced since meeting and following Jesus. A gifted tongue had Andrew, and because he was deep and complex in his approaches to philosophy and to sociology, a term not in common use in those times, he liked to try out his ideas on Ruth, who had a quick mind and facile tongue for learned expression. She who had studied in Egypt under old masters had no difficulty in understanding the trend of others' thoughts and was often two jumps ahead of them, understanding what they would say before they found words to express it. But Andrew was a match for her agile mind, and long were the talks they had together in trying to clarify all that they felt about Jesus and the path to salvation.

In rereading what the Guides had written thus far about Ruth, the alleged sister of Lazarus, I felt such admiration for her that I could not believe such a noble character could become a mere Ruth Montgomery after two thousand years. At the beginning of the next session I therefore asked, "Please tell me about the failings of Ruth. Surely she must have had some warts." I then meditated, murmured my usual prayer for protection, and placed my fingers on the typing keys.

Perhaps I should not have asked, because I could almost hear the cluck of Lily's (spirit) tongue as he responded: "The warts on Ruth? There were many, for she seemed capable of thinking of others only when she first assessed how it would affect herself. Even with Jesus, when she fled into the desert abandoning husband and children, she first thought of the adventure that it would be and the dramatic quality of becoming a follower, to rid herself of boredom in Jericho. She loved Jesus, yes, and had always done so, but primarily in relation to self, for first of all she had to love herself in order to see her love for others. Although we are expected to love self, she perhaps was too self-centered to appreciate that all others have separate lives from her own, for she viewed them only in relation to herself."

Oddly enough, I felt burning resentment at this puritanical analysis. Had not Jesus himself told his followers to abandon all others and follow him? Apparently reading my thoughts, the Guides continued with equanimity:

"Yes, Jesus told his disciples and followers to leave household and all others to follow him, and within that framework Ruth was simply anticipating his preachment. But in that lifetime she had come back to test qualities of self-submission, and again she

was falling down in her self-given assignment. Jesus, of course, was aware of her pledge when entering into flesh, and he wanted to help her keep that pledge. No, Ruth was not bad then, anymore than she is today. It is only that this particular soul is still fighting the old fogie Self."

Here again, then, was reference to Arthur Ford's earlier pronouncement in A World Beyond *that after completing one life span we review our mistakes and make a definite resolution to develop needed qualities such as humility, service to others, love, or thoughtfulness when we return to flesh.*

Mentally reviewing this lesson, I asked how Ruth happened to choose the household of Jeremiah into which to be born in Palestine, and the Guides replied: *"Arthur Ford has ever been a kindred soul to you in many earth lives and in the spirit realm. Often he has been a leader to you, and ever has there been abiding trust and friendship. Although neither of you knew, before entering the flesh in the Palestinian life, of the momentous events that would transpire while Jesus walked the earth as the Christ Spirit, yet were you drawn to Arthur in that embodiment. Because of that akinship you readily felt drawn to him when his wife Sarah was with child. This was at the start of his second family, remember, and you had previously known Lazarus, Martha, and Mary, who were likewise drawn to Arthur and Sarah and you, to round out the family circle."*

I felt that this was less than a complete answer, but I had to be content with it until months later, when the Guides began to discuss other alleged lives of mine that I have also shared with Arthur.

4

Beginning the Ministry

The image of Jesus I held in my mind's eye was a reproduction of a painting that hung on the wall of numerous Sunday School classrooms during my childhood. To me he was rather effeminate-looking, with delicate features and limpid brown eyes, except for a dark beard that covered the lower part of his face. Perhaps I was thinking of this one morning when I sat at my typewriter, to begin the daily session, because the Guides wrote:

From the time that the first disciples were gathered in Capernaum, a feeling of awe invaded all who came in contact with Jesus, the carpenter's son. He was of sturdy build, strong in leg and arm, and his torso was that of a young Amazon. He was approximately five feet seven or eight inches tall (people were shorter in those days than now), with light brown hair that hung loosely to his shoulders. His beard was unclipped, but it flowed in such natural contour that there was no shagginess to its aspect. It was light-colored, like the hair on his head, and soft to the touch. His eyes, at once piercing and penetrating, yet soft and compassionate, were of a deep blue. His teeth were strong and white, and his skin was bronzed from the desert sun.

When he strode among the people, his step was quick and purposeful, as if he were saying that there was much to do in a very brief time. A glint of humor lurked in the eyes, that were well-set beneath arched brows of brown with flecks of white from the bleaching of the sun. To his followers he had the face of an angel, yet to those who mocked him he seemed a too-perfect young man, although none cast doubt on his virility. *(Later I was to learn that Edgar Cayce had also said Jesus had "blue or gray" eyes.)*

Jesus wore cloth headgear during the daytime because of the strong sunrays, and except on special occasions he wore a loose-fitting robe whose sleeves were all of a piece cut as part of the robe so that two pieces of cloth were sewn together at the sides. His robes were sometimes beige and sometimes blue, and all wore sandals on their feet in those days.

Except for Ruth, the other children of Jeremiah (Arthur Ford) had darker hair and brown or green-flecked eyes somewhat like Jeremiah's own, as only she inherited her mother's coloring. Many Galileans were blond and blue-eyed in those days, and the mother of Ruth was originally Galilean. Ruth, the teenage girl of the trek from Egypt, was now a handsome woman of thirty and four. Her hair was still untouched with gray, and her blue eyes sparkled with intelligence and comprehension. She was of middling height for women of those days, approximately five feet and one inch, but lithe of build, and she walked with a quick, eager step as if to suggest that the next moment would be even more intriguing than the last.

At the time that Ruth knew Jesus again in the Jordan area his father was then passed on, but she remembered Joseph with warmth and respect, for he had ever been tender to Jeremiah's children as well as to his own. While Ruth and Jonathan were in Capernaum they went to see the mother of Jesus, and Ruth was delighted to find that age had dealt softly with the beautiful woman whom she had adored as a child. Mary, who still lived in Nazareth, was at this time staying with the mother of Peter in Caper

aum, and her blue eyes lighted with fond remembrance
s she clasped Ruth to her heart.

*Having seen paintings of Mary only as a young mother, when
'esus was a baby, I asked the Guides to describe her appearance,
md they wrote:*

Mary was now approximately forty-three, and her gold-
:n hair was shot with silver which glistened like a halo
n the Galilean sunlight. She was slighter than Ruth,
carcely reaching five feet in height, and her eyes were
s deep a blue as those of her son Jesus. Mary wore her
iair flowing, except when she went about her daily tasks,
t which time she tucked it neatly into a little blue cap
)f a material somewhat like today's denim.

"You have scarcely changed, Mother Mary," Ruth said
vith warmth as she looked admiringly at the woman who
vas only nine years older than herself.

"Ah, how womanly *you* have become," Mary replied.
'Ever were you giving of thyself to Jesus and thy father's
'oungsters. Often these days I have seen Lazarus, Mary,
nd even occasionally Martha, though that young woman
s seldom far from home."

Ruth sought words to express what was in her heart.
At last she said, "Mother Mary, how well it is with thee
hat thy son Jesus is the pinnacle of men, and all who
ind their lives changed by their meeting with him are
iffected for the better."

"Aye," Mary replied softly. "It is a mother's privilege
o accept all that she sees and hears about her son with
apture. He walks in grace."

For a little while they talked woman talk until Ruth,
emembering that Jonathan was waiting outside, beckoned
iim and presented him to the mother of Jesus. As Mary
urtsied, she saw the eyes of the man who was husband
o Ruth fill with wonderment, and before she had time

to assess the meaning of the glance, he was saying, "Mary Mary, most honored of all women, thou who art the mother of Jesus of Nazareth, how favored thou art of God that such a one should emerge from thy loins. Permit me, pray thee, to tell thee that I love him as my own being and in any way that I may serve thee, please know that such a time will be treasured forever by thy humble servant."

Mary softly replied, "The time will come, fear not, when all of us will be tested for our strength and our love of him."

In the days that followed, Ruth went often to see the woman whom she had loved since childhood, and sometimes Jesus joined them in the simple cottage where Peter's family dwelt. But Jonathan was growing restive to be so far from home, with little to do except talk with the followers. And when Ruth recognized the normal reaction of a man of business, she agreed to return to Jericho with him, having learned that she was not a free soul who could do as she wished, but must give thought to her earthly ties and obligations. They therefore gathered up their family and handservants and rented donkeys which carried them south along the fertile Jordan valley until they reached their home in Jericho.

On reading these words at the close of the session, I felt like uttering three cheers for good ol' Ruth. At last she seemed to be putting others before self, since obviously she would have preferred to stay where the action was instead of returning to Jericho. At least I, who loathe housework, would have chosen almost any course to avoid it. But what of Jonathan? Despite his spiritual "salvation," was he still putting self above service? Yet he did have a family to support and property to administer. The Guide made no comment on Jonathan's decision, but continued smoothly.

From time to time disciples stopped at their open door

o sup with Ruth and Jonathan, and exchange news of he growing movement; and occasionally they reported on demonstrations against the man Jesus and his followers. This evoked consternation, for was not Jesus the most holy of men, and had he not seen fit to spread the message of God's love throughout the land? Sometimes he had to go into hiding for a time, and once, when hired agents of the temple in Jerusalem sought to do him bodily harm, Lazarus brought Jesus to the spacious home of Jonathan for safekeeping. They rejoiced in his company, and Ruth wisely made no attempt to follow him when he went off into the hills to fast and communicate with his Father, God. For only three or four days did he tarry. Then, with word from Lazarus that all was at peace again in Jerusalem, he rejoined his followers beside the River Jordan and resumed his ministry.

With the twelve disciples selected and trained, Jesus then set forth through Galilee, but concentrated his efforts at Capernaum, for Nazareth still paid no heed and knew him not as the Son of God. At the synagogue in Capernaum he raised his sweet voice in praise of the Father, and to the amazement of the rabbis gave new insights into the scriptures as interpreted by them to the faithful. Some few questioned his teachings, but so logical were they to the people that resistance fell away, and they regarded with wonder this handsome young man with flowing beard and gentle manner who seemed to understand more than all the rabbis combined.

One day while Jesus spoke to those gathered around him near the wharf at Capernaum, a blind man knelt at his feet, saying, "Lord, Lord, I see thee radiant with light, though I have no sight. I know not why I was born blind, but I feel that if I am meant to see, thou hast the power to restore sight." The crowd hissed at him for demanding the impossible and seeming to test Jesus, but the Master placed his hand on the sightless eyes and spake thusly:

"Many are the ways to see, my man, and because you have
seen that which others do not, thy sight shall be restored
to thee. Rise and look about ye."

The man rose, then opened his eyes, and fell in a faint.
A murmur of discontent ran through the crowd of
onlookers, but in another moment the man opened his
eyes, gazed at the Master, who was viewing him with com
passion, and burying his face in Jesus' garment, said, "Lord,
Lord, thou hast given me that most precious of gifts, the
power of sight."

"Rise," said Jesus, "and go thy way, using thy restored
sight to the glory of our Father who granted thee this
gift." The man made his way easily through the crowd,
bumping into nothing, and when the people realized that
this was no longer the walk of a blind man, they fell with
one accord to their knees, chanting, "A miracle! A miracle!"

*For several reasons this account gripped my interest when I
read it after the session. Arthur Ford in* A World Beyond *had
indicated that to be born blind was a karmic situation, a self
imposed handicap in order to repay some harm that had been
done to another in a previous life or a refusal to "see" that which
was spiritually significant. But Edgar Cayce taught that the Law
of Grace can take precedence over the Law of Karma, if we
truly forgive ourselves and others. It would seem, therefore, that
because this man not only had faith but also "saw" the spiritual
light emanating from Jesus, he had earned the right to restored
sight. The next day the Guides continued with the narrative, writ
ing:*

In the days that followed, many ailing and doubting
who hitherto had scorned the man Jesus flocked to Caper
naum as word spread of the miracle. Some who were taking
the mineral baths at Tiberius rushed to the synagogue
and the byways of Capernaum, seeking the man who had
the power of healing. The throngs became so great that

the rabbis complained of desecration in the temple, and Jesus led the people into the wilds on the other side of Capernaum, where he talked to them of their Father and told them of the wonders of heaven.

"Are there truly mansions there, Master?" asked an elderly man who was not long for the earth.

And Jesus replied: "There are mansions there, yes. If there were not, I would have told you in the synagogue. But the mansions are also here on earth awaiting those who would follow the way of the Lord, for we are the ones who create the mansions or the hovels."

A murmur of disgust ran through the crowd. How indeed could they build mansions when they had no coin even for the tax gatherer? But Jesus, sympathizing with their misunderstanding, told them clearly, "We are as God, for He has given us the power to create that which we will. Should we desire beauty and harmony we have but to think it and live in the state of God's grace. Think ugliness and hatred, and we live with it."

Some were puzzled, but others in a flash of comprehension realized that this man was telling them that within each heart is the power of good or evil, beauty or ugliness, love or hate; and that to the extent that they cultivated the good, the tawdriness and disease fell away.

Intrigued by the reference to "harmony" as well as beauty, I asked the Guides for an elaboration, and they wrote: "There is a natural law of harmony that fills the universe, a feeling of oneness that melds together all who are warring within self and with each other. The best way to become attuned to this vital oneness is through meditation at the same hour each day. Think oneness. Feel oneness. Meld self into the whole of humanity and of the natural oneness of earth and sky and sea. There is a rhythm to the universe that all should feel as they go about their daily tasks. The subconscious recognizes this, and if one (through

*meditation) will bring it into his consciousness, each day will
pass more harmoniously, assuming purpose and logic."*

Since Arthur Ford in A World Beyond *had stressed that
we, through our thoughts and attitudes, create our own mansions
or hovels—our own heaven or hell—I felt that I had begun to
understand the meaning of the words the Guides attributed to
Jesus. They therefore continued:*

Many were the converts that day and in the weeks to
come, and throughout the area of Galilee the lame and
halt and blind and sick came to kneel before this man
who by stretching forth his hand seemed to have the magic
treatment for all ailments. Some who believed strongly
enough were healed even at the edges of the throng, for
such was their belief that the magic was wrought in them
without personal contact with the Master. Some fainted
and when revived, shed their crutches and strode manfully
about without limping.

Sometimes Jesus introduced his gentle mother to the
throngs, for at this time she was living nearby, and some
felt that by gazing on the radiance of her countenance
the hate and evil fled from their hearts and minds, and
they became followers of her son. Matthew, once the
dreaded tax man for the crown, had earlier undergone
such a conversion and was a full-fledged disciple, spreading
the new gospel and teaching wide and far. Peter and
Andrew were ever active with the throngs, and although
they had many questions of interpretation which they put
to the Master, they gained eloquence in answering questions of those who sought out their presence for greater
understanding.

*Thus far the Guides had barely mentioned the familiar Biblical
story of the loaves and fishes. I asked them about that miracle
and they replied, "That which seems as a miracle is the working
of natural laws." They said Jesus tried to awaken the people
of Israel to the knowledge that each had within his own reach*

"these magnificent gifts of the Father," and they continued: "How clearly he was telling them that it was within the power of each of them to achieve his heart's desire simply by tapping the inner source."

At this point it occurred to me that Arthur Ford had earlier warned to "think well" before asking God for something, as we were likely to get it, and it might not be something that was good for us. The Guides now wrote: "The story of the loaves and fishes illustrates this basic law, that the cup overflows so long as it is filled with expectation. When we anticipate God's bounty, and knowing that it is inexhaustible give freely to all who would be nourished, there is no lacking in supply; for ever the cup is filled so long as we believe that it will continue to be, and so long as we share freely without thought of repayment from others."

The Guides said this is a natural law and not a miracle, "For as a man casts freely his bread upon the waters it will return to him again and again. Think on these words." There was a long pause in the writing, before the Guides at last resumed: "Those who saw the multiplication of the loaves and fishes believed it to be a miracle, but those who ate from the baskets of bread and fish accepted it as normal, for not having known the limitation of supplies, they recognized their own need and accepted that which was given. To them it was a normal provision to satisfy the needs of the body; but those few disciples who saw the ever-growing amounts of these basic supplies, and who should have by then known the governing laws of nature, were so astounded that many years after the passing of the Master they continued to tell about it as a miracle. Even those nearest disciples were unable to comprehend that there is no limitation to God's bounty. We need solely to feel the need, to ask that it be supplied, and to accept with foreknowledge that it will be forthcoming. The more we give, the more we receive, for as the man Jesus and his disciples gave freely of their scant supply of bread and fish, so it multiplied faster than they were able to give it away."

The Guides could be spellbinders when they chose, and although I still could not understand how the "natural law" operated, I did feel the substance of their explanation to be that if we asked

*with expectation, while generously sharing, our needs would be
met. The Guides then resumed:*

For the time being the temple authorities were somewhat
quiet, waiting to see whether this phenomenon would wear
itself out and the people go back to their old ways of subservience to the rabbis. But as time passed and more multitudes flocked into Capernaum, they began to protest
among themselves, saying, "What manner of man is this
who supersedes our authority with the people and heals
them of their aches and pains? Surely it is a hysterica
manifestation of the crowds, and these ailments were only
in their minds."

Many agreed, but stirred restlessly as they remembered
that the blind were now seeing and the lame walking with
out a limp. They thus questioned themselves: Were such
impediments likely to have been only in the mind, that
this man would be able to say "go away" and the ailmen
would depart? Then word came from Jerusalem that unless
this man came there for questioning by the high priests
a stop would be put to his ministry. Jesus heard of his
summons with mixed emotion, seeing into the hearts o
the priests that they would attempt to stop his direct contac
with the people, and for a few days he went alone into
the hills on the far side of the Sea of Galilee to commune
with his Father, seeking guidance.

On the third day he rejoined the disciples. He would
answer the summons to Jerusalem, he said, but use the
opportunity to preach the new gospel in a leisurely trip
along the Jordan Valley. He therefore bade good-bye to
his mother and his new followers and set forth on foot
But the crowds followed, and at each wayside stop he ex
tolled the wonders of God and the road to salvation.

"Is it *this* road?" one asked, and Jesus replied, "Yea
it is the way of the cross." None understood his meaning
but all sensed that he was asking for sacrifice on this plane
in order to gain an abundance in the next.

* * *

This reminded me that in A World Beyond *Arthur Ford had stressed the importance of returning to flesh again and again to overcome physical hurdles. He said that because of these earthly challenges, a soul can make more rapid progress here than in the spirit plane, where all automatically recognize and obey universal laws. Thus, we should regard the barriers here as stepping-stones to spiritual advancement.*

After a time most of the followers returned to Capernaum, their jobs and families. Jesus and his disciples pressed onward, finding new crowds along the way, and as they crossed through Samaritan country Jesus expounded the philosophy of brotherhood among men, saying that all have one Father in heaven and thus are brothers each to the other. This disturbed some of his followers, particularly the more orthodox Jews among them, but the Samaritans listened in awe, wondering what strange type of man could possibly pretend that they were the same as the other Semites who held forth in Jerusalem and Capernaum.

A woman at a well was lifting a bucket of water, and when Jesus asked her for a drink (for he was thirsty), she drew back in alarm, saying, "Sir, know you not that I am a Samaritan, that you ask me for water?"

And Jesus replied, "Yea, that I know; but know ye not that we have the same Father?"

"How could that be?" she scoffed. "For my father has seven children and you were never one of them, or I would have known you."

And Jesus spake, saying, "Yea, but your father of whom you speak is also my brother, and his grandfather was my brother, and all whom we see wherever we go are our brothers or sisters, for there is but one Father and He is the God of us all."

Then she understood that which he intended, and

although it was a new idea to her, she said, "But what will others say when they see ye drinking from my pitcher?" And he replied, "Love one another. Speak good to those who utter evil, and give thy heart to God."

She marveled at his way of speaking and asked wonderingly, "What manner of man are ye that you spread revolutionary words among the people?" And he said, "Woman, I knoweth thy life like an open book. I know that you cohabit with one who is not your husband and that fornication is a way of life with thee."

At this she drew back, blushing with shame that a stranger should know of her inner ways, but he said, "Nay, it is not to condemn but to point the way that I speak of these things. Even such a one as you is beloved of our Father, and as you turn from evil ways to trusting in Him who gave us life, wilt thou be blessed among women."

And the woman set down her pitcher and sobbed into her hands. But then a strange peace came over her, and she said, "Lord, Lord, I knew thee not when we talked, but now I have been given a revelation. Permit me but to touch thy garment and I will go to my home, there to break off old associations and begin anew, to serve as a handmaiden of the Lord God."

And the disciples watched from afar as she, a Samaritan, knelt at the feet of the Master and then rushed across the way to spread the word of the mysterious stranger who talked of God as if He were a friend.

Sometimes the writing style of the Guides seemed irksome and ponderous to me, but occasionally their phraseology was luminous, and I delighted in their expression, "the mysterious stranger who talked of God as if He were a friend." That gave me something to think about.

5

Reformation of Two Marys

At this time I left for the States, to make a television tour in connection with my latest book. On my return, the Guides seemed scarcely to have missed me, because the next morning they resumed the Palestinian story precisely where they had left off, writing:

As they journeyed along the Jordan toward its mouth in the Dead Sea, a runner came from Jerusalem, saying, "Who is Jesus of Nazareth?" The disciples moved to protect the Master, but raising his head from meditation, he spake, saying, "I am he."

The runner exclaimed excitedly, "Many people are massed before the temple in Jerusalem, demanding that the priests permit you to preach to them there."

"What sayeth the priests?" Peter asked impetuously. And the runner replied, "A welcome is being prepared, and he will be permitted to speak. I am asked to extend the invitation in behalf of the priests of the temple."

The disciples were overjoyed, but Jesus spread forth a hand, saying, "Be not hasty in thy celebration. I will go apart and pray." In a short time he returned, saying, "This time we shall enter Jerusalem, for my time is not yet at hand."

John, the youngest disciple, who had rejoined them that day after putting some affairs in order, embraced the Master, saying, "We understand not thy meaning, Master, but wherever thou goest, there will I go also."

That day Jesus preached near the spot where John, his cousin, had baptized him. The next night he spent at the house of Lazarus, en route to his meeting with the priests in Jerusalem. At the home of Lazarus a woman came who had been sick with the bleeding for many years and was frail and ready to drop. But when Jesus spake a word and placed his hand on her shoulder, the misery fled, and she arose with renewed energy, praising his name. And Jesus said, "Speak praise only of Him who sent me to minister to thy needs and those of others. Go thy way, for thou art healed, and remember to hold and cherish Him in thy heart."

Mary had long been missing from the home of her brother, and Jesus sorrowed; for although Martha explained that Mary was visiting kinsmen in Jerusalem, Jesus knew within his heart that harm had befallen the playmate of his childhood. The next morning Jesus and his disciples descended toward Jerusalem over the Mount of Olives, and after pausing in the Garden of Gethsemane to pray, they went on foot across the Kedron Valley and in through the shepherd's gate.

This was the episode to which I referred in the Foreword. A skeptic by temperament and training, I am always on the alert to check the Guides' assertions wherever possible, and I could find no reference to such a gate on the maps of Jerusalem. From my visit to the Holy Land many years earlier I recalled several gates to the city, but not until I now scanned numerous reference books did I learn that the only gate that gives direct access to the Kedron Valley was called, at the time of Christ, the Sheep Gate. Nowadays it is St. Stephen's. To return to the Guides:

None recognized Jesus and his disciples until they reached the square before the temple, where many were gathered, and one man shouted, "Here he is. I have seen him before, and this is the man who performs miracles."

Excited shouts arose from the crowd, and the priests came forth to view this person about whom they had heard so much from their flock and from agents in Capernaum. Jesus was asked, "Have you brought your magic potions with you?" And he replied, "Within my heart is the God of Israel."

The priests looked shocked and wondered if this were blasphemy, but Jesus continued, "That same and only God is within the hearts of all of us, and with Him all things are possible."

"Then heal me, Master," a beggar pleaded, holding forth his gnarled hands, which were crippled by arthritis, "so that I may work again."

"Ezekiel," Jesus said, "art thou willing to work for thy livelihood if God delivers thee from this affliction?"

"Yea, Rabbi," he replied. "I was a worker in stone, and now I cannot hold the heavy tools of my trade."

"Then thou art healed," Jesus said, lightly touching the drawn hands, and as the man released his curled fingers, they were as straight and painless as those of the Master. Sobbing with emotion, the man fell at the feet of Jesus, saying, "Thou art Lord most high! And to think that I sought to provoke thee, for believe I did not, but thou art indeed the son of God for whom Israel has long waited."

The crowd swarmed closer for a sight of the healed hands and then cried, "Hosanna." The priests, somewhat subdued by the demonstration, invited Jesus into the synagogue to preach, and there the crowds followed, intent on his words and speaking wonderingly in whispers of his mighty works.

When the writing ceased, I asked the Guides if others could develop healing powers, and they responded: "As to healing, any talent that has been highly developed during a series of lifetimes is available as a natural gift to those who return if they wish to use it." They then surprised me by declaring that I have innate healing powers that could be developed if I would put my mind to it, and that I should begin by concentrating on sending warmth to my fingers. Presumably this method could be used by others as well. At the next session the Guides took us inside the temple at Jerusalem and opened their dissertation with the speech that Jesus was delivering to the priests and the crowd of curious.

"Keep not the farthing that belongs to another," Jesus told them, "and to the priests give their due share. But whenever there is more than enough for thine own mouths, share generously with thy less fortunate neighbor, for we are all children of God, and He has provided enough for all. Give honor to thy parents, who were God's tools in thy physical creation, and remember that the little children who hunger for thy love and attention are mirrors of our Father and equal in His sight with thee. Go forth and love thy neighbors, not just the ones who are kindly and generous to you but also those who would steal thy bread if thy back were turned, for they are all a part of the Godhead, and are as thee in the sight of God."

"How could it be," a priest interrupted, "when we are bade to do good works, that those who do evil are equally loved by Jehovah?"

"We do not love the evil in those men," Jesus replied, "but we are bid to love the Godpart in each person, and thus to help him, through love, to shed those habits and ways of thinking that are not of God's design. Love is a healing force that binds all wounds and mends all hearts, so that by loving those who do not seem to merit it, we assist them in casting off the filthy raiment and emerging as clean as the river stones in the Jordan."

Breaking in, a man named Ephias asked, "Wouldst have us love a wife who has committed adultery with another?"

"Hast thou committed adultery?" Jesus replied, with a question that went straight to the man's heart. Then Jesus continued softly, "Would you have your wife take you back when you have lain with another? Then forgive her equally, for are you not both children of God, who yearns that both of you follow in His way?"

How interesting to note that in those days before women's liberation, when Palestine was most certainly a "man's world," the Guides have Jesus decrying a double standard for men and women. But far from recommending loose sexual habits, Jesus seemed to be warning that physical immorality, like other bad habits, degrades one spiritually. Arthur Ford had warned in A World Beyond *that unless we shed habits of overindulgence here, we are apt to become earthbound in the next stage of life, and to reincarnate with even worse habits. The Guides, after commenting briefly on sexual misbehavior, continued:*

The service was then disrupted by a sound at the open doorway, and several temple officials thrust a woman to the ground, saying, "Here, Jesus of Nazareth, is an example of that precept. Gaze on this woman who has committed adultery, and then we will punish her in accordance with our Mosaic laws."

The woman lay sobbing and bleeding where the soldiers had thrown her roughly onto the cobblestones, and as the crowd rushed out to gloat at her misery, Jesus stepped forth from the temple, saying, "Woman, hast thou sinned in the sight of God?"

She covered her face, weeping the more, and in a muffled voice replied, "I have lain with a man who was not my lawful spouse." And Jesus, sensing within his heart that this was the beloved Mary of his childhood, said, "Arise, for God our Father forgives all who repent, and thou shalt sin no more; of that I am sure." Tenderly he assisted Mary to rise, and when some members of the crowd murmured angrily that she should be stoned, Jesus said, "Let him who is without sin among you cast the first stone." Then he walked forth with Mary, and together with his disciples he took her to the house of her brother in Bethany.

On arriving there, Mary, who had spoken scarcely a

word since the encounter outside the temple, threw herself into the arms of Lazarus, saying, "Forgive me, a sinner, for I am truly repentant." Jesus said naught, and after a moment of hesitation Martha, in a quiet manner, asked her younger sister if she might draw water for her bath. Mary, sensing forgiveness in the tone, gladly assented and followed her to another room, where she bathed and changed into fresh clothing.

Ruth, who had been summoned earlier by Martha when Mary did not return home at the appointed time, came in from the garden. And because of the sweet understanding between the two sisters, Ruth soon heard the full story from the lips of Mary. Ruth then realized that her little sister had strayed from the fold, not out of wickedness, but because of her unsatisfied yearning for Jesus, who would never be her spouse. Thus Mary had sought to dampen the fires within her loins by taking other men, but the fires would not be quenched because the element of love was lacking. Now Mary knew, in an abundance of regret and self-searching, that only with the quality of love would she ever find solace in the body of another. Thus she pledged her life to God and to His Son who strode the earth, mindful that spiritual love far surpasses that of the fleshly pleasures.

At this point I asked how spiritual love, or love in the spirit world, compares with love while in physical embodiment, and Arthur Ford replied: "The power of love is the greatest that any soul experiences: love of God and love for others. To love is divine, as the poet said, and how true it is, for that is the one quality above all others that binds spiritual beings together in flesh as well as spirit. The satisfaction, however, is far greater on this side (in spirit), for here it is as a magnet which unites souls so closely as to be unknown in physical body, where each travels the road alone. Here it is possible to be truly united with another in blissful oneness."

Ruth remained for a time at the house of Lazarus, devoutly intent on learning at the knee of the Christ, so that she would better be able to bring his message to those others whom she and Jonathan sought to teach. She sent a messenger to bring Jonathan, and for several days they dwelt there while Jesus taught them many things. He taught that the body is the temple of the living God, and that we must keep it clean and ready at all times to receive the Holy Spirit.

When Mary heard this, she cringed and slunk away. But Ruth found her, and after Mary had sobbed on her shoulder, Ruth said, "The Master tells us that each day that we live in perfect wholeness is as if we are born anew, so put aside that which cannot be changed, little sister, and henceforward view thyself as a newborn babe, white as the snow of Jerusalem, for if God forgives us, what matter if man think ill of us? Thou didst make a mistake, true, but never wouldst thou have done so if thee had fallen in love with another fine young man instead of the Lord Jesus, so that you would have married him and borne his progeny. Think not ill of thyself, sister, but start a new day that is free from sin and temptation."

When Ruth returned to the gathering, Jesus smiled his approval, as if he had divined in some mysterious way all that she had told Mary. Jonathan discussed with Jesus the successes he was having in bringing the message of salvation to those in and around Jericho, and even as far away as Philadelphia (present-day Amman), where his business had taken him. And he sought answers to some questions that had troubled his listeners, such as: "What happens after death?" and "Why were we born?"

Jesus replied that we came into flesh to demonstrate our willingness to assume burdens in the name of the Father and to resist temptation. The hurdles, he said, are the measure of our strength and are never higher than we have the ability within us to surpass.

"Never did our Father give us greater problems than

we are able to solve," Jesus said, "or heavier burdens than we are able to support. And as to death, that word was invented by the Devil to frighten man or lull him into believing that the grave is the goal, for in truth there is no death. We continue to be 'us' through all eternity, and though we die many times in the flesh, we return evermore to the land of many mansions, where all may live in harmony unless their own mind and spirit have created huts and hovels for them instead."

Zebedee, the father of James and John, asked if heaven were a long way off in the sky, and Jesus replied, "Are you not in heaven now, supping with loved friends and partaking of good-fellowship?" Then Ruth sensed that heaven and earth are as one, except that the soul inhabits the one with body, and the other with spirit only.

This statement recalled Arthur Ford's amused assertion in A World Beyond *that "We're not up there someplace, or out there. We're* here." *He went on to say that as I sat at my typewriter each morning, letting the Guides write through me, we were much closer than we had been in the days when Arthur and I chatted in my living room in Washington, D.C.*

At the next day's session the Guides returned to the scene in Lazarus' house and the discussion with Jesus, writing:

The disciple John asked, "Master, Master, why is not dear Lazarus one of thy twelve disciples who travel with thee?"

After exchanging a smile with his oldest and best friend, Jesus said of him, "Lazarus has known whereof we speak on all things since early boyhood. He needs no training from me, and although his responsibilities to his sisters keep him oft here in Bethany, Lazarus would be ready at any time to lay down his life for our Father. Of this I am aware."

Lazarus threw Jesus a glance of pure and unselfish love

as he replied, "Aye, and were the Master who abides with us here today at any time to command, not only myself but the sisters of this household and Ruth and Jonathan would gladly forsake all to follow him. And gladly would we die for him, for he is far dearer to us than a brother. He is a part of our own souls."

The following morning Jesus set out with his disciples en route to Capernaum.

The vivid scene brought to mind the story of the fig tree. I remembered from childhood that the incident was said to have occurred near Bethany after Jesus and his disciples paid a visit to Jerusalem; and since it had always seemed out of character for Jesus to damn a tree because the figs were out of season, I asked the Guides about it. This is their reply:

"The fig tree incident is purely symbolic, for Jesus knew when fruit is due and when it is not. By the telling of that parable he was demonstrating that any good we do bears good fruit, whereas those thoughts and actions which are evil will shrivel the tree (our souls) and cause barrenness in our spiritual growth. You know that the stories in the New Testament were passed on by word of mouth for a long time before they were written in the form we know them. Someone manufactured the tale that the tree to which Jesus pointed then withered and died, for Jesus was using it only as a dramatic example, and he attempted nothing beyond that. If the tree died it was a natural occurrence." To return to the narrative:

En route to Capernaum, Jesus and the disciples were passing the outskirts of Tiberius when they heard sobbing and the loud cries of a crowd. Rounding a corner, they saw a woman brutally thrown into the dusty street, while cursing throngs surrounded her to stone the woman. A priest, recognizing Jesus of Nazareth, thought he saw an occasion to test the young man who seemed never to be hesitant or confused, so he held up an arm for the crowd to stay the stones while he looked, arms akimbo, at Jesus, saying, "Well, young master of the rabble, what would ye have us do with this woman who has passed from brothel to brothel, selling her wares and cheating the wives of their husbands' favors?"

The woman lay sobbing into her arms, her face hidden and her body covered with grime from the street. Jesus wrote with his forefinger in the sand, and when the priest looked curiously at this response, he read, "If you have not sinned, then throw a stone at her."

Taken aback, the priest turned and left the scene in dismay; and as others of the crowd began walking around to read what Jesus had writ, they also walked away, until only the woman was left with Jesus and the disciples.

"Whom fearest thou, woman?" Jesus asked at last. "The crowd has departed. Where do you reside?"

"In Magdala, Lord," she replied.

"How do you call me Lord when we have not met before?" Jesus asked. And she replied, "Thou art my Lord and I will follow thee to the ends of the world, for I have heard of thy wonders, and if thou wilt permit me to accompany thee, I will serve thee evermore."

"Come," Jesus said, "and we will take thee to my mother, who awaits us in Capernaum." And they walked the remaining miles around the lake.

This episode, as I indicated in the foreword, perplexed me until I later read that Edgar Cayce had also spoken of two adulterous Marys whom Jesus rescued from angry crowds. However, Cayce identified Mary Magdalene as the sister of Lazarus; and I am inclined to go along with the Guides at this point, instead. It seems less logical that Lazarus and Martha, living in Bethany, should have had a sister Mary who came from Magdala, at the far end of the Jordan River above the Sea of Galilee.

Meanwhile, in Jerusalem the priests were furious that

they had allowed Jesus to escape their clutches. Not even to themselves would they admit that they had been so over-whelmed by his presence that they were loath to lay hand on him. Now, without his radiant presence, they were able to think more clearly and to evaluate the threat he posed to them and their office. "Stop Jesus" became their theme song, so to speak, and after a time they began to lay elaborate plans to bring him to heel. *(This paragraph seems so full of modern slang that I suspect Arthur Ford was dictating it.)*

On one of these occasions when they met to lay their evil plot, a man among them ventured to inquire, "But what right have we to seek vengeance on this religious leader of men?" Scarcely were the words uttered than others pounced on him, raging that he had fallen under the spell of the man from Nazareth. And well they might suspect it, for had they themselves not felt the spell of his presence?

Thus silenced, the man named Joseph, who was of Arimathea, said no more. But when next he heard that Jesus was preaching in the area of the Dead Sea, he slipped off from Jerusalem to alert the Master to the possible threat against his life. Jesus, regarding him with infinite love, thanked him for his consideration and asked what he could do for him in return.

"Master, I have an epileptic child whom none is able to heal," he responded. "Wouldst thou see him, if only to satisfy me that I have done all that can be done for this precious one?"

"And why me?" Jesus asked. "Surely there are healers in Jerusalem who would be glad to aid the child of a high priest."

Joseph of Arimathea replied, "Master, none but thee has such power, for thou art surely the Son of God."

Then Jesus said, "When you return to your home in Jerusalem tomorrow, take these two hands of yours which have held mine and lay them tenderly on the shoulders of thy son, letting the thumbs come together above his throat. And when thou hast done thus and spoken in reverence the name of our Father, thy son will ail no more." And when Joseph returned to Jerusalem he did as directed, and from then on, his son never suffered another seizure.

Although the Bible makes no reference to this alleged incident, and I cannot vouch for its authenticity, it could be an interesting explanation of why, after the crucifixion, this same Joseph made available his own unused tomb for the body of Christ.

The band of Jesus' followers was now spreading out in many directions, meeting sometimes secretly and at other times addressing gatherings. Ruth and Jonathan were among them, as were some who had been healed and others who had fallen under the spell of his ministry. Mary of Magdala was attracting attention by her good works and gentle ministry to little children who needed healing. The home of Lazarus was ever open to those who sought food and inspiration, and many were the weary souls who paused there, thinking life had lost its meaning, only to go forth refreshed and kindled with a burning desire to better the lot of mankind.

When the two younger brothers of Jesus were able to leave the family business and go abroad in the land, they were hailed with awe by those who believed Jesus to be the Anointed One. Timothy, James, and Judas went as far as Damascus and Tyre to spread the glad tidings that the savior of the world walked with them in Judea and Galilee, and Thomas was also speaking. Andrew, who was particularly eloquent, took the good tidings to Petra and beyond the Euphrates, and whenever he returned, he brought word of those who yearned to hear the Master and would come as soon as they could find someone to watch over their business. Thus the word was spreading far and wide, and though Jesus was a symbol of purity within the realm, he was anathema to the high priests, who felt threatened in their authority.

Ruth, too, was doing some soul-searching. It had cut deeply into her heart to learn that her sister had been a wayward girl, for she had been more nearly mother to her than to Jeremiah's other children. She began now to show more personal interest in her own two daughters, taking much time for their lessons and their spiritual growth, and the girls opened up like flowers to their mother, who hitherto had seemed too busy to have much time for them. Thus a closeness developed, and when Ruth and Jonathan traveled to spread the good news of Jesus' ministry, the girls were invited to accompany them; and they made friends throughout the area, for they were attractive and well behaved. One was nearly a woman now, while the other was nine or ten. The girls loved particularly to go to Jerusalem, which was truly a sight for them after the limitations of Jericho.

From the time that Mary of Magdala joined the followers of Jesus until the end of his physical life, she was like unto a shadow to our Lord, going wherever he went and ministering to the needs of him and his disciples. She dedicated her life to him as completely as if she were the first nun, who gives herself as bride to Christ in the church of these latter days. The relationship was without evil, and so selfless did she become that all sin was washed from her, so that she shone as a saint.

Surely this holds meaning for all who in youth commit serious indiscretions. Through repentance and atonement they are able to wipe clean the slate and rid themselves of karmic indebtedness. The Law of Grace supersedes the Law of Karma.

Ruth came to know Mary Magdalene well, both during Jesus' ministry and thereafter, when Mary made her good works felt throughout the land, aiding the sick and suffering, and succoring to the needs of the little band of followers who for a period after that terrible time at Golgotha were left leaderless, frightened, and adrift.

Another whom Ruth knew well was Judas Iscariot, who had been a tanner of hides and a tradesman in Judea before laying down the tools of his trade to follow the path of Jesus. He was a rather purposeless young man until the message of Christ penetrated his heart, and he became convinced that God dwelt within all men. He felt that he was cut out for leadership, and for a time he was totally dedicated, utterly devoted to Jesus and the miracles that he was able to perform. But at times he resented the other disciples, some of whom, like Peter and John, seemed closer to the Master. He was unable to understand that by pouring out their love in such enormous quantity to Jesus, Peter and John were naturally receiving back in the same measure as they gave.

Even of Mary Magdalene was Judas resentful, for he felt that the conversations Jesus exchanged with her could better have been used in schooling him to become a leader of Judea. Jesus sensed the unrest within the heart of Judas, though he spake not of it, seeking by loving devotion to erase that which was evil within him. On one occasion Judas spoke directly to his problem, saying, "Master, if thou art indeed he whom God has promised to send among us to save Israel, why then dost thou not march into Jerusalem with thy hundreds of loyal followers and let us proclaim thee King of the Jews?"

Jesus, somewhat amused by the preposterous proposal, but reading into the words Judas' own lust for power and acclaim, replied, "Judas, Judas, thou knowest that we seek not power but purity, not lust but love. Of what benefit would a kingship be to our work, when God the Father is our King and we are endowed with his love?"

Judas shrewdly replied, "But Master, how much easier

and faster it would be to spread the word of God's message if you were in a position of high authority in Jerusalem, where all would have to listen to thee and hearken to thy words."

Jesus replied softly, "A little child will lead us, for by such purity of thoughts and deeds we find entrance to the kingdom of heaven on earth." Judas, feeling himself mocked, sulked angrily, saying no more. But as Jesus departed, he placed a hand on the shoulder of the seated Judas, saying, "Hearken, brother, lest we confuse worldly power with the eternity of God's kingdom." Then he went away into the desert to pray and ask God, if it be His will, to lift up the heart of Judas to the ecstasy of grace, so that he might envision the true glory of God's pathway.

I shuddered to read about Judas, the anathema of the Christian faith—the one of the chosen twelve who betrayed Jesus! How did he get that way? I asked the Guides for information about Judas in some previous incarnation that was influencing his Palestinian one, and they wrote: "Judas in a life in Arabia was a prince who dealt sternly with all who challenged his authority. Not such an evil one, but arrogant and self-assertive, brooking no interference and considering himelf above all others with whom he came in regular contact. He had particularly disdained fishermen then, and in the Palestinian life he subconsciously felt scorn for Peter, Andrew, James, and John and was jealous of their place in the affection of Jesus, whom he truly revered, innately recognizing in him one who was far greater than himself. He wished Jesus to declare himself in full authority to the Jews, and was disgusted that he was willing to walk about on foot with a group of ragged fishermen, rather than sit in the highest authority in Jerusalem, where Judas could be his right-hand adviser. Not a pretty picture, but a human one; and Jesus felt compassion for his aspirations, even as he tried to explain the spiritual value of serving others rather than being served." The Guides then continued:

On another occasion Judas argued with Peter, and when Peter rebuked him for worrying too much about worldly goods and not enough about inspiring sinners to repent, Judas harshly demanded, "And have I not heard some of you saying that you will sit on the right and left hand of Jesus in the ultimate seat of glory?"

Peter, his face flaming angrily to match the color of his hair, replied, "Surely you realize that John and James were jesting about who would have the favored seat, for would we presume to outguess our Heavenly Father at the judgment seat?"

Thus, there was occasionally dissension among the disciples, but since Judas traveled widely, particularly in the western provinces and beyond Damascus, he was not too often in their midst to be a real fomenter of dissatisfaction.

Troubled by still another reference to the judgment seat, I asked the Guides to explain why the Biblical characters spoke so often of it, whereas Arthur Ford and Lily have insisted that we judge ourselves. This was their reply: "We quote in this material what was said in those times, when all Jews of the faith believed in an ultimate judgment day, at which time the chosen would sit at the right hand of God. This still pervades Judeo-Christian belief today, but we have told you that we are our own judge and jury, shutting ourselves off from the grace of God until we have amended our errors and devoted ourselves to love of others."

The Guides seemed to be agreeing with Biblical scholars that the Old Testament presents a vengeful God, intent on punishing His chosen people, whereas Jesus brought the message of a loving God who yearns for all to be saved.

6

The Age of Miracles

Arthur Ford and the Guides, while dictating material for A World Beyond two years earlier, had skipped from one subject to another so frequently that I encountered difficulty in assembling their message into order and sequence. By contrast, they now seemed so "carried away" by the Biblical story that it flowed freely, in perfect continuity, and I interrupted their narrative only to ask for further elaboration on particular segments. I had the feeling that if my own strength had been sufficient, they could have dictated this entire account of Jesus' ministry in one sitting. But I have repeatedly cautioned others to devote no more than fifteen minutes a day, at the same hour, to automatic writing, and the Guides have respected my wishes by limiting themselves to that amount of time. Their typing pours forth through my fingers with astonishing rapidity, but after approximately a quarter-hour it ends abruptly with the words, "This is all for now." On this particular morning, they began:

On the day of the Passover that year Jesus and his disciples worshiped in Capernaum, and many were the miracles that Jesus performed for the throngs of people who came from around Galilee for the observance of the feast. Beggars and cripples, the lame and the blind found new life in the presence of him whom God had sent in healing ministry. The disciples marveled anew at his power and asked of one another, "When will you or I be able to perform such service, for has not the Master told us that all which he does we will be able to do also?"

Jesus, reading their thoughts, called them to a grassy place and spake: "You who have abandoned farms and homes and ships and all else to follow me are blessed among men, for He that sent me among you has granted your wish to mend the ailing, and for this remaining time of my ministry I will promise thee such power as thou hast never known. Peter, do ye not see the blind man sitting against yon tree? Test thy new powers on him."

Peter asked eagerly, "Lord, what will I say to him, and what will I do?"

And Jesus spake, saying, "Worry not about thy gift of tongue or thy power to administer to others, for when the time cometh, all will be given unto thee by thy Father who is in heaven."

Peter strolled across a little glen to the man who seemed sleeping against a tree, and as he stretched forth his hand to him, the spirit of the Lord entered Peter and he said unto the man, "Seeth me?"

"Nay," the old man replied, "for I am without sight."

And Peter, with the Father speaking through him, said, "With those two eyes wilt thou see, and with new energy wilt thou rise and follow the man who sent me hither."

The old man, with new sight swimming before his eyes, leaped to his feet, saying, "I see ye, but know ye not. Where is this man who sent thee to me?" When Peter led him toward the group surrounding Jesus, the old man fell on his knees, exclaiming, "Hosanna! Thou art indeed the son of God whose fame has spread before thee." And he rushed through the town crying that now he could see, and that all lameness had departed from him.

Then Peter saith unto the Lord, "Master, Master, pity my unbelief, for now I am like unto a man reborn. Never again will I question thee." And Jesus smiled sadly, for in his heart he knew that the time was not far off when Peter would deny even having known him.

* * *

In recent weeks the Guides had made frequent reference to Jesus' ability to read another's thoughts, and now they were having him see into the future. I therefore requested an explanation, and they wrote: "Jesus had clairvoyant powers that he received as a gift from the Father at the time that he merited reception of the Christ Spirit. (This, they said earlier, came at the time of his baptism by John.) All may develop this clairvoyance to a degree, and saints and master teachers have had it throughout history, to a degree unmatched by most of us. It is a quality to be developed as one opens oneself, through meditation, to increased spirituality."

Then John, the youngest disciple, said, "Lord, will I too one day have such power as Peter?"

And Jesus said, "Yea, for the power is not Peter's, but belongest to our Father who grants all things to those who follow in His way."

John thereupon walked forth to a cripple hobbling along the roadway, and stretching forth his hand, said, "Old man, why limpest thou?" And the man answered, "Because one of my legs was broken in my youth and never mended properly."

John, feeling the charge of energy entering his body, commanded, "Look thou at thy leg. I see no fault in it."

The old man looked down in amazement, for the bent and withered leg was now as straight and perfect as his other; and jumping with excitement, he too went rushing back to the town.

Then Jesus filled all the disciples with the power from his Father, and they went forth to heal as well as to administer to the souls of those who gathered from far and near.

Aware that numerous people today such as Kathryn Kuhlman,

Oral Roberts, Olga Worrall, Mr. A in Born to Heal, *and many primitives in Mexico, Brazil, and the Philippines seem to have healing powers, I asked if there is any correlation between their gifts and that of the disciples. The Guides responded: "The disciples, having devoted themselves to God and His son, were able to receive the gift of healing without further effort at the spoken word of Jesus. Yet there are thousands, perhaps millions of people living in physical body today who are able to develop that gift and to become a transmitter for the Lord. All who unselfishly wish for the ability to heal others are able to discover this natural law, and one way to begin is by meditating on the subject. Concentrate on feeling the healing power entering each finger, accompanied by radiating heat; and as the power enters, use it only for good."*

Now came a man from Damascus who had heard of Jesus through the apostles, and when he found himself in his presence he fell to his knees, crying, "Master, my assets are many, but my soul hungers for that which only you can provide. Teach me, O Jesus of Nazareth, to live in such harmony with others that my servants will not annoy me and my benefactors not burden me with their complainings."

Jesus spake, saying, "And what is the cause of thy dissatisfaction?" The man, who was called Calias, responded, "The world is wearisome with so much getting and spending, and though I rush hither and yon in search of peace, I find it not."

Jesus looked deep into his soul and asked, "Art thou running from thyself?"

"Why, Master, what a question!" the rich man exclaimed. "How would I be so foolish as to run from myself when that is an impossibility?"

Jesus said, "How long, Calias, since thou didst look within to find the seat of thy discomfort?" And the man said, "How could I look within when my eyes are at the front of my head and looketh only outward?"

Jesus replied, "Ah, but the sight of which I speak is the greater one, for it looks within and without and all about, and when one learneth this sight he has no need for other." And with that the man found his sight vanished, and he fell down in confusion, saying, "Jesus, my sight is gone."

"No," the Nazarene replied, "thy sight is only now beginning," and calling Peter to his side, they assisted the man to walk to Peter's home, which was nearby. For two days the man rested in a small room on a pallet. And Jesus taught him to meditate, so that the sight within him opened wide, and he saw clearly that his problem was too much of the world's goods and too little of divine understanding.

Here I asked for fuller elaboration, and the Guides wrote: "Practicing meditation while in physical body advances the soul rapidly, bringing one closer to the life force and universal rhythm. This puts self in attunement with the divine plan, which is perfect oneness. When the art of meditation is developed to a high degree in the physical plane, advancement in the next stage is more rapid. Otherwise it will have to be learned here in our plane, at the beginner's stage." Many books are available on various methods of meditation, and I devoted a chapter to the subject in A Search for the Truth. *To return to the man who had lost his physical sight:*

Thus, when his sight was restored to him on the third day, he arose a wiser, stronger man. Returning to Damascus only long enough to dispose of his properties and leave fair shares to those of his children who had need of them, he returned to become a trusted and enlightened follower of the Christ.

Thomas, ever a doubting man, did not think that Calias would return empty-handed, but on seeing the transformation in his face, he fell on his knees before him, saying, "Thou art a more worthy man than I, for thy sacrifice is greater than mine."

And Calias contentedly replied, "I know not of what sacrifice you speak, for I am born anew, even as a baby enters the world without aught to clothe him."

What a good lesson this seems for all of us who think that happiness lies in amassing wealth and fame, rather than in discovering the inner peace that comes through serving others!

On the day following the Passover celebration in Capernaum, Jesus and his followers walked westward to a mount that has a broad view of the surrounding countryside. Along the way Jesus healed several lepers, and when he went to the top of the mountain to pray, he took three of his disciples with him, asking the others to remain below and heal those in the crowd who continued to swarm about them. It was a steep climb to the crest, and when they reached it, Peter, John, and James threw themselves full length on the ground to catch their breath. Perhaps they dozed off, for they were aroused by a brilliant light, and standing within the radiant center were Moses and Elias with Jesus.

A voice from out of the universe spake unto them, saying, "This is my beloved son in whom I am well pleased," and the three apostles were struck dumb with awe. They saw the three saints conferring, and they scarcely dared breathe for fear they would vanish. At last Peter cautiously asked Jesus if they might prepare quarters for his guests, but Jesus shook his head, saying, "Have ye not heard of the communion of saints? They will tarry but a little while, and when they are gone I will have but a short time more with thee."

The disciples withdrew a little way, so that Jesus might talk in confidence with Moses and Elias, and such peace overcame them as they had never known. It was as if already they rested in the bosom of Abraham, and although they tried desperately to stay awake and view the tableau so brilliantly illuminated, their eyes became heavy. Once again they slept. When they awakened, the scene was a normal one. The spirits had vanished, and Jesus was resting with his back against a large stone.

"Master, where art thy hallowed guests?" James ventured. And Jesus replied, "Always they are here, but thou lackest the ears to hear and the eyes to see them."

"I see them not now, Master," John protested. And Jesus smiled at the beloved disciple, saying, "Ah, how young you are, and what a long path you have ahead of you. Come, we will be on our way." And they descended the mountain while Peter pondered the meaning of the Lord's words.

Recalling the chapter in A World Beyond *in which Arthur ford discussed the six higher planes of consciousness through which soul must pass before achieving perfect oneness with the Creator, asked how this process applied to Moses, Elias, and Jesus. They hose not to answer in full, writing only:* "As a soul advances through the different realms or planes and endures the vibratory influences of other planets, he at last reunites with the Central ore of God. Jesus, after his crucifixion, had no need for this additional process, since he had previously, between lives, traversed ll of those planes except the last. By voluntarily returning to hysical form to demonstrate his victory over temptation, he became e Christ, and upon his physical death could return directly to od."

A few days later Jesus set forth through the land of ne Samaritans, a surprising number of whom were pledging their lives to the new testament as delivered by him. o great were their numbers that, although Jesus and the isciples were expected at the home of Jonathan and Ruth for a feast in their honor, thence to proceed to Philadelphia where Jonathan had arranged for the Master to address a large group of converts, he tarried for a time with the Samaritans.

He reached the home of Jonathan a day late, and such numbers of followers accompanied him that instead of a beautiful banquet to be served in the loggia for the honored guest and apostles, Ruth had to share the feast with the multitudes who camped outside the house and had no other place to find food. Thus Ruth viewed her carefully planned dinner as a failure; but Jesus comforted her saying, "To give a banquet for honored guests brings no spiritual reward, for while others hunger, none should enjoy his meal. By sharing thy largesse with those who hunger for enlightenment as well as that which fills the stomach, thou givest to God our Father as well as to the guests."

Ruth hung her head in shame at these words of righteous wisdom, and Jesus assured her that the way to the kingdom of God was through the stomachs as well as the hearts of the needy, for as we share, we grow in God's grace.

"How much should we give, Lord?" Ruth asked in perplexity. And he said, "There is no need to ask, for then numbers would be given openly. Let not thy right hand know what thy left hand does, and vice versa, so that no numbers are kept and no thought given to what thou does for thy fellow man. Let God keep the books, and free thyself from the burden of remembering, for be assured that all is registered in the heart of God, and not one iota escapes His watchful care."

Since this was another reference to the akashic records, I asked if the Guides cared to say more on the subject, but they gave me a rather mocking reply: "You know perfectly well that the akashic records contain all data since the beginning of time

"But what if one gave everything away and had nothing left for himself?" Ruth inquired. And Jesus said, "Does a sparrow store up treasures to be hidden in his nest? Nay, God provides for His sparrows, and would He provide less for thee whom he created in his own Father-Mother image? Think not to store up treasure, for so long as God is in His rightful place, there will He watch over thee."

Ruth looked in mortification at her large wardrobe of carefully stitched robes and sandals, and gathering them into her arms, walked among the people outside the house, giving to one this and to another that. And when Jonathan observed her activities, he too sought out his chamber servant and had him distribute his clothing. Then they went with Jesus, Andrew, and John to Philadelphia, while Peter, James, and Bartholemew turned toward Jerusalem, where they had business in the city.

In reading those paragraphs, I wondered how literally Jesus meant the instructions about living as the sparrows, giving no thought to tomorrow. From my travels in the Orient I am aware that some men, giving everything away, have donned saffron robes to live as mendicants, simply holding out a bowl to receive charitable offerings of food. But what if everyone did likewise, and we became a nation—a world—of beggars? Frankly, it made no sense to me, and I had a sneaking suspicion that after Ruth and Jonathan gave away their clothing, they purchased more, rather than go about in rags.

My own feeling of guilt persisted, however, and after eyeing my wardrobe I removed a number of dresses to be distributed for charity. Yet I must confess that I gave only those articles of apparel I had not worn for some time and probably would not need again. Another question still plagued me: What would most of us do today if a bearded, blue-eyed stranger spoke to us in the streets saying something like, "Leave thy possessions and thy family, and follow me"? Jesus sent home the Palestinian

Ruth when she tried to do just that. On the other hand, I have
known people who gave so freely of what little they had that
their cup seemed always to be overflowing. It is a puzzler!

Musing about this feast which Ruth had prepared for Jesus
and the disciples, I was prompted at a later date to ask the Guide
a question that has long intrigued me: Did Jesus eat meat?

"Yes," they replied, "for in those days there were still sacrifice,
in the temple, and people were accustomed to the killing of sheep
and fowl for sacrificing as well as eating. Jesus was not a veg-
etarian, and we find no record of his having commanded people
not to eat meat."

Runners had alerted the converts in Philadelphia, and
a large throng swelled the plaza as the group reached the
center of the city. Jonathan had provided donkeys for
Jesus, the three disciples, and his own family; but many
others followed on foot a part of the way because they
could not bear to have Jesus out of their sight. A rabbi
invited Jesus into the synagogue, and as many as could
do so crowded in after him, while others waited in the
plaza. Inside, Jesus asked the eager listeners, "Dost thou
believe in the indestructibility of God?"

"Yea," some murmured.

"Then knowest thou that each of us is indestructible.
For if we are parts of God, and He Himself is indestructible,
then how would it be possible for a single one of us to
perish?"

"But what of hell?" a rabbi demanded. And Jesus replied,
"Ye have read of the 'eternal' fires of hell, so even that
is not destructible. But why concern thyself with hell? For
unless one chooses it as his preferred sphere of activity,
he has no need to be there."

Shocked, the rabbi persisted. "But what choice do we
have, for it is Jehovah who decides which of us goes to
heaven and which to hell."

And Jesus replied, "Think thee not that our Father is a *just* God? He would not condemn us to hell unless we had chosen it, as evinced by our activities. It is we who decide whether to live out our days in torment or in peace and grace. Each day of our lives we are making that choice. Yea, in each moment of the day; for were we to select the way of God, we would each moment be thinking of others, lending a hand to their suffering or need, and thanking our Father for the opportunity given us to serve our brothers and our neighbors and all who pass before our door. Have no fear of the fires of hades unless thou desireth to go there, through worship of that satanic majesty who rules over the nether region and cordially invites you each moment to enter into his realm.

"Be it in thy nature to prefer the company of Satan to God, then thy choice is an easy one. But hearken to these words. God does not give up easily, for like a good shepherd, He pursues his lost sheep with tender solicitude, and whenever thou dost pause to listen to the inner voice of conscience, it is God crying to thee for thy soul. To each of us He hath given the knowledge of good and evil, and even as a bird flies true on its course, should we not do likewise? It would be a foolish bird indeed who deliberately flew head-on into a wall or a fire. Take heed, then, to that still voice within that tells thee thou art only one of the billions of creations of our Father, with all others as important as thyself. For I say unto you that not one will advance his own salvation unless he has helped others along the path with him. We are parts of our Father and He of us, and we need each piece to make a perfect whole."

I remembered the words Arthur Ford had used in A World Beyond *when I asked him about Satan. "There is a devil," he wrote, "but not as man conceives it. The devil is the force of evil which has been gathering in the earth since man first trod* it in *physical form.*" Arthur claimed that the devil was "never a person, but a force so powerful that it gathers strength with each new wrongdoing, just as good shines forth more brightly with each kind and thoughtful deed." He added that "Man, not God, created Satan," and that Satan is "fed by every evil thought and activity."

The Guides continued with Jesus' address in the synagogue and then wrote:

Afterward Jesus strode outside, and holding up both arms in a graceful gesture of blessing, told the crowds waiting in the plaza to follow him to a shaded area on the outskirts of the town. There he preached to them for the remainder of the day and part of the next. And Jonathan noted with satisfaction that of all those to whom he had personally spoken during his travels to Philadelphia, not one failed to come and kneel before the Christ, asking to serve in his name.

Was Jonathan, I wondered, exhibiting a bit of too-human pride? The Guides did not comment.

7

The Healing Ministry

Imperceptibly, Lily, Arthur Ford, and he Guides were changing my own attitudes toward life. I was becoming increasingly generous with material things, but now became aware of restless stirrings within. Should I not also e giving more of myself? Since the age of seventeen, when I began working my way through Baylor University while serving simultaneously as a reporter on the Waco (Texas) News-Tribune, *have regarded* TIME *as the world's most precious commodity.*

There never seem to be enough hours in the day! Yet through self-discipline and hoarding of time I have managed to write books, give lectures, make tours, manage a household, and still somehow answer the hundreds of letters that arrive weekly from readers of my books. Since moving to Cuernavaca with my husband four years ago, numerous members of the Episcopal Guild had been urging me to begin a meditation-study group, but I had repeatedly pleaded lack of time. Always it seemed that I was either writing a book or flying to the States for television promotional tours of the previous book.

Now, inspired by the words attributed to Jesus about service to others, I began conducting a weekly meditation group, passing on what I had learned in similar classes and helping the members to interpret their dreams. To my surprise, I find that the experience is enriching my own life as much as it is those who attend. There's that "overflowing cup" again!

In dictating the material for this book, the Guides did not bother with dates, but one morning I was perplexed to read, "On the day of Pentecost . . ." Surely, I thought, that is a purely Christian observance which would not have been celebrated until after Jesus' physical death. The Guides must have erred! Referring to a dictionary, I read that Pentecost is indeed "a Christian festival commemorating the descent of the Holy Ghost upon the apostles.' But to my immense relief I also read that Pentecost far predates the coming of Christ, being "a Jewish harvest festival observed on the fiftieth day from the second day of Passover."

The Guides were therefore correct, and this chapter begins fifty days after the disciples, according to the Guides, received their gift of healing through Jesus at Capernaum, although the Christian festival dates from the day that the disciples "spoke in tongues' after the crucifixion.

On the day of Pentecost Jesus and his disciples were in Jerusalem, and at the behest of the crowds who heard of his identity he consented to speak in the tabernacle

"Tell me not," he said, "that thou art sons of Him who created the heavens and the earth, for until ye have cast off thy garments of self-indulgence and given thyselves totally to Him, ye are not fit to inhabit the earth that He created with the Word. Know ye not that the Father knows thy every thought before it is translated into deed? Understand ye that the rich are not privileged to sit with the Father? For having already received their reward in the earth they will not fulfill that which is written: that only the poor and the pure in heart will sit beside the Father in His eternal kingdom."

The people looked at each other in disgust. This was not that which they came to hear.

"I tell ye," Jesus continued, knowing their thought, "that until you have shared thy abundance with thy less fortunate brothers and have freed those whom thou dost treat as lowly servants, ye cannot enter into the kingdom of God For when one owneth that which is actually the Father's and calls it his own, he has no liberty to place himself on a pinnacle and say 'do this, do that' to others.

"He it is who will be the slave when he crosses over to what man calls the hereafter, for the first shall be last and the last will be first. It is written that the meek shall inherit the earth, but I tell thee that the heavens shall be inherited by those who in this life bow down to their Father and love their fellowmen. Give of thyselves generously, for in giving one receiveth; and unless one demonstrates his love of the Father by loving those of His creation, he will not step foot into the promised land beyond the grave."

When the writing ceased and I read these passages, I was reminded of what Arthur Ford had written two years earlier, shortly after his death. Turning to A World Beyond, *I read in the chapter "Proper Preparation" about the joy one experiences in the spirit world on learning of his spiritual advancement through "insignificant deeds" he had forgotten, such as the helping hand extended without thought of personal gain. Conversely, he is disappointed to discover that the largesse he had bestowed, for which he had received publicity and praise, counted for nothing on the other side. Ford's explanation: Why expect reward in the afterlife if we have already had it while in physical being? The moral, he said, was never to let the left hand know what the right hand does.*

The next morning the Guides returned to the tabernacle in Jerusalem, where Christ was speaking by invitation, writing:

Then Jesus told them the parable of a man who sowed seed lavishly, wishing to harvest a mighty crop. But the winds came and blew away all that fell on barren ground, and the birds ate that which fell into the crevices of rocks, and so little fell on fertile soil that the crop was scant. Yet that which lived and grew became the mightiest grain

ever sown, for the master tended that which remained
with such devoted care that not one grain was lost or permitted to wither away.

"Thus it is with our Father when the seed which He
sows begins all of an equality," Jesus said. "Some nurture
the seed that falls on good soil, while other seed is cast
away by the winds and left on barren rocks. I say unto
you that unless you provide within self the rich and nutri-
tious soil to receive the grain, it shall be denied thee
forevermore." Some of those who heard these words
wriggled uncomfortably and began looking within themselves, but others dismissed it as mere verbiage and
departed to resume their lives of barren waste.

Then Jesus led the disciples to a place high on the roof
of a house and said to them, "When my time is at hand
thou wouldst remember this place, for we shall here have
a covenant." The disciples wondered at his words, but
none dared ask the meaning, and they went with him to
the place of Gethsemane, where they rested under trees
and gazed back at the fair city of Jerusalem, high on its
magnificent hill.

"Lord," Philip asked, "was there ever a more beautiful
city than holy Jerusalem?

And Jesus replied, "From afar it has a good and sparkling
air, but within its bowels are dark passages and sinful people; people who know *of* God, but know not God, and have
no wish to learn His ways. They will perish and the very
birds of the air will find nothing but desolation below,
for Jerusalem shall be destroyed stone by stone, and the
evil of its ways will be remembered for ten thousand times
ten thousand years."

Peter asked, "Master, is there no way to prevent such
disaster? For there in Jerusalem is the tabernacle of thy
ancestor David and his handiwork."

And Jesus said, "Not in stone is the word of God written,

but in the hearts of men. Until that day cometh when all men are of goodwill to one another, the earth shall be devastated by famine and floods, war and earthquake, and all manner of destruction; for that which the Lord made He will as easily take away. So keep thyselves pure in heart and free from lust, for to those who love God there is no destruction, only eternal life."

The disciples soberly pondered these words, knowing not quite what to make of them. After a while Jesus rose, and followed by his disciples, walked over the Mount of Olives to the home of Lazarus, who received him with great joy. Ruth and Jonathan soon arrived from Jerusalem, where they too had gone for the Pentecost, and that evening all sat about an open fire, filling their hearts with the wonderment of Jesus' words, for he talked freely of the days to come when strife would be ended and a new beginning made in the hearts of men.

"Not in this lifetime," he cautioned them, "but in other lifetimes to come will you know this wondrous change, as man puts aside his evil ways and rejoices with the Father."

This seemed to be a direct reference to reincarnation and to a time yet to come when mankind will actually realize peace on earth. But whether Jesus actually spoke these words attributed to him by the Guides, I have no way of knowing.

When they returned to Capernaum, Peter went to see his mother-in-law, who was ailing, and finding her with a burning fever, he asked Jesus to see her. Immediately upon his laying a hand on her hot brow, the temperature returned to normal, so that she arose and prepared a meal for Jesus and others of the disciples who were there. Peter was a widower, his wife having died in childbirth along with the baby many years earlier, before he knew Jesus.

While in the vicinity of Capernaum Jesus spent some

time with his mother in Nazareth and with his brother and sister who still lived there, although his other brother now lived in Capernaum, where Mary often visited.

"Son," Mary said one day, "it filleth a mother's heart to overflowing to hear of thy good works and see with mine own eyes the tower of strength that thou hast become."

Placing an arm lovingly around her shoulders, Jesus replied, "Couldst help but be a good man with such a mother as thee?"

"Would that thy father Joseph had lived for this day," Mary said softly, "for he always took such delight in thee."

And Jesus said, "Yea, but thou knowest that he is awake and aware of what we are doing, and all of us have the same Father in heaven who knows each time a sparrow drops."

"Son, hast thou given thought to marrying? So many women love thee, and I think what beautiful grandchildren would be mine."

Smiling down at his mother, Jesus said, "How like a woman to be matchmaking! Have ye not sufficient other children to satisfy thy wish for grandchildren?" Then turning serious, he continued, "It is not for me, Mother, to join my life with another's, for it belongs in this life totally to Him who sent me to do His work. Mine is to love all in such manner that each knows I am a part of him and he of me and our Father. With a wife that would be impossible, because of the special family relationships. Fear not, Mary my mother, for thou shalt be blest with grandchildren, but not of my issue."

At least the Guides seemed to be "humanizing" the relationship of Jesus and his mother. The Bible records few exchanges between them, and I have always felt somewhat repelled by the fact that in speaking to her, the Gospel accounts have Jesus addressing her as "Woman" in a somewhat chiding way.

Now in the days when Jesus walked the earth, the Pharisees were highly aroused because they saw the popularity of the man and the worshipful attitude of his followers, so they began scheming to do away with him. At one point they tried to ambush him on the road between Capernaum and Nazareth. Another time they tried to entrap him with the priests in Capernaum, but to no avail, for Jesus knew of their designs within himself and was not willing to be captured until God told him that his mission in physical body was at an end. Thus he seemed to live a charmed life, and the Pharisees eventually gave up the schemes in favor of something which would have a more legal flavor than outright murder along a highway.

Not all the Pharisees were bad men, remember, but simply narrow-minded and determined that nothing should undermine their hold on the people. Some believed honestly that theirs was the only way to truth and light, while others were jealous of the popularity of this strange man who had come out of Nazareth to preach and teach. On one occasion they sent a member of the Sanhedrin, disguised as a lowly peasant, to attend one of his meetings near the Dead Sea. But instead of reporting back to them in indignant tones, the man became a convert and thereafter followed Jesus, becoming one of the larger group known also as disciples. Another time the rabbis at Capernaum sought to entrap Jesus when they interrupted one of his discourses to accuse him of violating the Sabbath.

"Thou hast practiced the magic healing on the Lord's day when it is forbidden," they expostulated. And Jesus replied, "If one of thy flock were dying on the Sabbath, would ye refuse him thy blessing or the services of a doctor?"

The rabbis looked affronted, and Jesus continued, "If

a shepherd found one of his sheep caught in a fence and starving, would he fail to release him on the Sabbath? Even so, God permits His healing work to be performed, and surely it is more blessed on His day than any other."

Here again it seemed apparent that many of those in authority genuinely believed that Jesus was employing magic or trickery. Otherwise they could scarcely have been so obtuse. Even today the American Medical Association seems to take a remarkably insensitive attitude toward those who effect healing without use of scalpel or pill.

The rabbis dared not argue further, since it was obvious that the people were with Jesus, and after he left the synagogue, he walked only a short distance before a child came screaming down the street, with his father in pursuit. The man fell exhausted at the feet of Jesus, saying, "Rabbi, what shall I do about my son, who is possessed by demons, so that he foams at the mouth and runs amok?" The child had stopped a short distance away and stood hissing, but when Jesus held out his arms, he reluctantly drew nearer, then suddenly leaped into his arms, moaning and sobbing.

"Little one, why weepest thou?" Jesus asked tenderly. And the child sobbingly replied, "Because I know not what possesses me to do evil, for I truly want to be good."

"Then thou shalt at this moment be rid of all evil things," Jesus said. "Go, my child, with a heart full of love, and remember that thy wish hath made thee whole." To bystanders Jesus explained, as the child skipped away, "The Father waits only for us to ask in true humility. Ask and ye shall receive."

"Lord, what if I asked for a million denarii?" a man said with a grin.

"Ah," Jesus said, smiling. "How would you ask for that in true humility?" And the crowd laughed, understanding the joke, for sometimes Jesus spoke in such oblique parables that they were beyond the comprehension of the throngs. Mary Magdalene stood near John in the crowd, and when Jesus noted her smile, he remarked, "How easy it is for one to be happy when he basks in the pleasure of God."

The episode with the child reminded me of a question that has long plagued me. Since there are no Gospel references to house pets, I asked the Guides whether Jesus liked animals, and whether there were any incidents to demonstrate it. They replied: "As to animals, Jesus adored the fleecy, flat-tailed lambs that made excellent pets before they reached maturity, and he often used them in his teachings as examples of gentleness and tenderness. He yearned after all forms of life as gifts from the Creator and walked fearlessly among all animals, even wild ones, as if they were his brothers. Often did he stoop to pet dogs and cats, a gesture so normal with him that none thought to add it to their accounts that were passed along to those who later wrote the Gospels."

During this period Jesus and his followers spent most of their time in and around Capernaum, for the trading season was in full sway and many were the people from other lands who were passing through that busy center. At times Jesus went out on the boat of Zebedee with James and John, and the two disciples noted that whenever Jesus was on board, the fish were abundant.

But widespread dissent began arising against Jesus' teachings. His listeners seemed more interested in his performing miracles than in heeding his sobering words, which taught that those who follow the narrow path are beloved of God. The Jews had been taught fear of God, but Jesus brought the word that it is equally important to love God and one another, and some of the earlier followers fell away, refusing to share with the less fortunate. Others of course replaced them, but the movement at this time was not growing substantially.

Jesus, praying alone on the other side of the Sea of

Galilee, saw a vision one day of a turtle creeping slowly along the way, beset by obstacles it had to surmount or go around. But steadily onward plodded the turtle, until at last it reached the sea. When it did so, it lifted itself by magical wings and flew across the water, there to find peace in a land so rich that it never had to crawl again.

When Jesus described the vision to his disciples, even Thomas the twin finally grasped its meaning, that by sturdily pressing ahead on the narrow path, overcoming obstacles and never complaining that the load is too heavy, one wins eternal bliss by lifting oneself at the day of death to the promised land, God's kingdom.

This parable seemed in keeping with the Guides' earlier assertions that more rapid progress in spiritual growth is made because of the hurdles we can overcome in the flesh. Thus we should be grateful for the obstacles, rather than resent them.

Ruth and Jonathan came to Capernaum to report that although some of those in Jericho and Philadelphia had become backsliders, many others in villages beyond the Jordan had pledged their lives to Christ and were sending contributions to the work and the sustenance of Jesus and his disciples. Thus heartened, the disciples gathered beside the lake at sundown, and after partaking of fish and bread, Jesus told them the story of the leper who waited outside the gates of a rich man's house, daring to go no nearer but desperate for food. When the rich man rolled by in his carriage, the leper begged, "Food, oh, lord," through lips partially eaten away by the terrible disease. The servant, who was driving the carriage, lashed out at the beggar with his whip, striking him across the face, but the rich man stopped and ordered the servant to carry the man back to the house for treatment and food.

"But, lord," the servant said, cringing, "I too will contract the dread leprosy if I carry him." The rich man replied,

"Then you will know how it feels to be lashed across a face that is already half eaten away." And he forced the servant to take up the bleeding man and carry him back to the house.

"Now, what would you do in such a circumstance?" Jesus asked around the circle.

"I would probably have left the employ of the rich man, rather than touch the leper," one in the crowd said. And another answered, "I would have been careful not to touch him except through the clothing, and then I would have burned it."

Ruth said, "It is true that the servant should have been punished for lashing the face of an already woefully suffering man, but I do not think the rich man had a right to order the servant to come in direct contact with the disease unless he himself were willing to touch or help carry him."

"Ah, you have anticipated the outcome." Jesus smiled. "That is exactly what happened, and because the rich man, who had been without fault, also helped carry the leper, God took pity on the little group. The ailing one was almost instantly cured, even as they were transporting him, and neither the master nor the servant contracted the disease, though the servant had a scar resembling the lash of a whip across his face for his remaining life on earth."

Late into the evening they talked beside the quiet waters, and in the morning Ruth went to see Mary, the mother of Jesus, before departing on a long journey to Thessaly. The two women embraced fondly, and Mary with a prophetic air declared, "I fear that this is the last supremely happy time we shall meet, dear Ruth, so it makes me doubly glad that you are here."

"But why, Mother Mary?" Ruth asked. "Of what is thy foreboding?"

"Only that when the wind is blowing sweetest, an acrid quality suddenly seeps into it, and I want to weep. Within myself I know that my son Jesus will not linger long with us here and that evil lurks at the corners of our happiness."

Ruth tried to reassure her, saying that Jesus would do well to travel only in the middle of sturdy groups, so that no harm could befall him. But Mary shook her head, saying, "That which is to be will be, and God's will be done."

Then Ruth returned to the group for final farewells before she and Jonathan would sail for Thessaly.

8

Lazarus Comes Forth

Assuming that the Guides would begin the next day by discussing Ruth's trip with Jonathan to Thessaly, I thought I should find out where in the world they were taking "me." Turning to the dictionary, I read that Thessaly "was a former division of ancient Greece." Thus primed, I was ready for the journey. But the Guides have a will of their own, and after completing the morning session, I learned that they had instead plunged into the thrilling episode when Lazarus was raised from the dead. This is how they began:

One day Jesus was meeting with his disciples on the eastern side of the Jordan when a messenger came, saying that his friend Lazarus was seriously ill with the fevers, and he was urgently needed in Bethany. Jesus, on receiving the news, withdrew to a quiet place and knelt for a long time in prayer. During a part of his communication with God, the disciples saw him in seeming agony, as if he were being given an unhappy task, but when he returned to their circle, he made no comment. Since he gave no sign of imminent departure, the disciples were puzzled, for they thought they knew how great was Jesus' love for his oldest and dearest friend, Lazarus.

Jesus began quietly to discuss with them the plan for a larger group of disciples, approximately one hundred twenty-five in number, to be sent as teachers throughout the greater area of Asia Minor. At last, unable to bear the suspense, Philip interrupted to ask, "Master, art thou not going now to Lazarus in Bethany?"

Tears sprang to Jesus' eyes, but he firmly suppressed them and merely shook his head in the negative. Peter, bewildered and puzzled, said, "Wouldst have one of us go, Master, to try the healing power thou hast given us?"

There was a long pause before Jesus replied, "Men of destiny, when the time hath come we will all go to Bethany, but the waiting is hard."

None could fathom his meaning or the cause of the delay, since they were doing naught that could not as well have been discussed in Bethany. Had the two men quarreled? But no, Jesus would never have permitted a disagreement to imperil the need of his friend. Then why? The next day a second runner arrived, begging Jesus to hasten to the house of Lazarus before it was too late. The runner said it was impossible to reach Ruth or Jonathan in time, since they had already sailed for Thessaly to spread the message of Jesus to Jews in that area.

Still Jesus made no move to depart, and another day passed before he at last signaled his disciples to gather sustenance for the two-day trip by foot to Bethany. They were still a good way off but in sight of Bethany when another runner reached them to say that Lazarus had been dead for several days. Jesus said naught, and his disciples were afraid to look directly at him, but they could sense the terrible misery of his being. They pressed on silently until they reached a certain resting place not far from Lazarus' house, and there Martha came to meet them, saying, "Jesus, Jesus, had you come when I first sent for you, my brother need not have died."

Her reproachful manner and doubt of him so moved the Master that he wept. Martha, seeing with shock what she had done to one whose manner was ordinarily so calm and tranquil, also wept, and kneeling at his feet, said, "Master, forgive me, for thou knowest what is best, and whatever thy power is, thou knowest how best to use it."

Jesus asked about Mary, and Martha told them to rest awhile, for there was no longer any need for haste, and she would send Mary to them with refreshments. Returning to her brother's house, which was crowded with friends who had known and respected Lazarus, Martha found Mary and told her that Jesus had finally come and was pausing at the usual resting place in a grove of trees just off the roadway to Jerusalem.

Mary gathered up some refreshments, water, and clean cloths and sped along the path. There she flung herself at the feet of Jesus, saying, "Why is it, Master, that thou healeth all others, but not thy beloved friend Lazarus?" Then, seeing the stricken look in Jesus' eyes, she said, "Master, forgive me. Thou wert doubtless on the Lord's business and could not get away."

She began hastily to bathe his hot and dusty feet, and when Jesus stood refreshed to complete the journey, he took the young woman by the shoulders, and looking down into her eyes, said, "Mary, our Father's ways are not always the ways of man. Believe me, I would have come at the first message of his illness, but our Father had greater designs and bade me wait until He gave the signal for me to come. Now I am here, and we shall go to see thy brother."

"But, Jesus, my brother has lain dead these several days," Mary protested, thinking he had not understood the message of his death.

"Aye," Jesus replied. "We must rouse him." Frightened at the odd words, Mary rushed ahead and signaled for Martha to join her away from the crowd at the house. Jesus led the disciples to the tomb where Lazarus had been laid away, but word of his arrival could not be kept secret, and the other friends and mourners also came out to the tomb along with Mary and Martha.

Here the words that Arthur Ford had written in A World

Beyond came vividly to mind: "My son Lazarus was not buried alive, but did indeed die and come back to life, regardless of what the scoffers say. I was with him on this side and then watched as he returned to physical body to prove that all things are possible if God wishes them to be done." Now I could scarcely wait to read the next installment, which began:

"Roll away the stone," Jesus commanded his disciples, and when Martha protested that the flesh would be rotting and fetid by now, Jesus held up his hand for silence.

When the rock had been rolled away, Jesus stepped to the mouth of the tomb, entered briefly, and in a loud voice commanded, "Lazarus, come forth." Murmurs of indignation ran through the crowd, but were superseded by gasps when Jesus stepped forth followed by Lazarus, who was firmly wrapped in his burial raiment.

"Undo his bindings," Jesus said to Martha, for Mary was weeping so that she would be of no assistance.

To my delight, the following morning Arthur Ford took over the narrative, writing:

Martha, ever the practical one of my children, immediately untied and unbound him. Lazarus had been with me on this side for several days while pondering the absence of Jesus, since we on this side do not automatically know everything the moment that we become spirit instead of inhabiting flesh.

Lazarus had been awake and aware on this side, but puzzled that his friend would have let him die without an attempt to save him. He had not yet developed the ability to enter another's mind or to penetrate through closed doors.

Thus, when Jesus entered his tomb, Lazarus thought it was simply the visit of a grieving friend, as we viewed it from here. He was therefore as astonished as I when Jesus commanded in that ringing voice, "Lazarus, come forth." It was such a command as I have never heard, and in that instant Lazarus returned to his body and found himself on his feet, for the supernatural quality of the command left no question of being disobeyed.

One moment Lazarus was here with me, and the next he was in the body that was stiffly walking out of the tomb. I can vouch for his death as firmly as for my own, because he was here with me until the call came from Jesus.

I have no comment on this extraordinary account because I am as stunned by it now as when these words were first dictated through my typewriter. Many things in this book astonish me, but none as much as this particular incident. When the writing resumed, it was the Guides who were again collaborating.

Word spread rapidly that Lazarus had been raised from the dead. Too many eyewitnesses had been present to allow for any mistake in the circumstances, and because Jesus was now the talk of Jerusalem and the adjoining countryside, priests of the temple met again to plot the drastic measures that would have to be taken. Since the Passover would be observed in a few weeks, they decided they would wait until the city was full of pilgrims, with Jesus surely in attendance. Then they would bring his case before Roman authorities in order to demonstrate the blasphemous quality of his activities. That, at least, was their thought.

During this intervening period Jesus and the disciples were busily engaged in spreading the good news of God's supreme powers and the authority that had been vested in his son Jesus. Even sorcerers and magicians were now being converted to the new way, for although they had seemingly duplicated some of his feats heretofore, even they had to bow down before a man with the power to return life to the dead. Many of them abandoned their trade and became followers of the ever-expanding band of devotees, and as the disciples moved about the country on both sides of the Jordan River, they were overwhelmed by the numbers of new adherents to the way of truth.

Often Jesus stopped by to break bread with Lazarus and his two sisters in their home. Ruth and Jonathan were still traveling, and although word had been sent to them of the miraculous revival of Lazarus, there was now no need for them to hurry home, since he was as well and strong as ever. One day Martha made bold to ask Lazarus in the presence of Jesus how it had been on the "other side."

"Were you sleeping or simply in a state of suspension?" she asked her brother. And after exchanging a twinkling smile with his friend Jesus, Lazarus replied seriously, "I was with our father."

Eagerly she asked, "You saw God?"

"Nay," he replied. "I speak of our father Jeremiah [Arthur Ford], who kept me good company during those few days after I departed my body."

"Lazarus, tell us more!" Mary said breathlessly. "How is our wonderful father?"

"Wise and well," he replied, "for he lives and knows and is as aware of us as we are of each other."

"How could that be," Martha prodded, "when we see him not and hear him never?"

"Ah," Lazarus replied, "but he sees and hears us, for he is far more alive than we are here."

"How does he come here?" Mary asked. And he continued, "There are no barriers on the side of death where he is now. I was not made aware of all the possibilities of the spirit, since I was there so briefly and was just beginning to adjust to the fact that death is nonexistent. But our father, Jeremiah, was telling me of the wondrous things they are able to do, and in a while longer I might have become an apt pupil of that wisdom."

"Is this true for everyone?" Mary asked, turning to Jesus.

And his blue eyes lighted as he replied, "For all who love the Lord and willingly labor in his vineyard."

"What of those evil ones who turn their backs on good deeds and refuse to help others?" Martha asked. And Jesus said, "For them the sleep is long and the misery tortuous, for having been made aware of God the Father in this life, they are doubly beset by sin. Those who have never heard the word of truth are like half-developed blossoms that wither and drop off while the plants send out new shoots at a later time. But those who are fully developed and have heard the good word of everlasting life, yet heed it not, are thus shorn of their bloom and left to suffer their own torments, until at last they learn to return good for evil and to love their enemies. This may take many lifetimes to accomplish, for the way is long and the load is heavy. I would not return those souls to the flesh, as my Father gave me the power to do with Lazarus, for they need lengthy coaching in the next stage before again returning to take up the task of living in physical form."

Arthur Ford in A World Beyond *had indicated the importance of remaining in spirit until a soul has thoroughly assessed his previous errors and resolved to undo them, before reincarnating. He said many of the rioters and hoodlums in today's world are those who rushed back into physical body too quickly, without taking time on the other side for proper contemplation.*

"Tell me, dearest brother," Mary asked Lazarus, "were you glad to return to the flesh after those days with our father, Jeremiah?"

The question embarrassed Lazarus, with Jesus at his side, but the Master said with a smile, "Say that which is in thy heart."

Lazarus after a brief hesitation said, "It was peaceful there, and beautiful, and the opportunities for learning were so great that I was eager to plunge into the activities.

But have I not often said that I would give my life for our friend Jesus? Then how could I also fail to give my death for him? At his command I returned, as effortlessly as a baby nurses at his mother's breast. There was no hesitation, no holding back. Suddenly I was here, and because there was not even time for a choice, I well knew that it was God's will for me to return. Now I am glad to be among you, my loved ones, and I thank Jesus for his handiwork."

"Not mine but our Father's," Jesus reminded gently, and then they turned to other subjects.

Familiar as I am with Arthur Ford's descriptions of what transpires after the process we call death, I nevertheless feel some embarrassment at the ease with which the Guides have Lazarus discussing his in-and-out-of-body experiences.

I am also troubled by the direct quotes that they frequently assign to Jesus and his mother, Mary, believing that some readers may resent the effrontery. Yet I am a reporter, not a censor, and I am therefore permitting them to tell their story in their own way.

9

The Resurrection

The morning after the Guides completed their dramatic account of Lazarus' return from the grave, they effortlessly picked up the thread of their narrative about Ruth, writing:

Meanwhile, as Ruth and Jonathan, en route home, sailed around the island of Crete, word reached them that Lazarus had died and been resurrected from the tomb by their friend Jesus. Their amazement knew no bounds, and Ruth fell on her knees to thank God for sending His beloved son, who had proved such a loving friend to her family and all of Israel. Hailing a passing ship that was sailing directly for Judea, they sent a message thanking Jesus for preserving Ruth's beloved brother. Then, minds at rest, they continued their voyage to ports where they were spreading the word of the Master's work and receiving contributions for him from a number of pious Jews.

On this homeward journey they were in good spirits until on reaching Mesopotamia, they heard whispers about a plot in Jerusalem to put an end to Jesus' ministry by violence. Hastily sending a warning message ahead, they cut short their stay to begin the long overland trek to Jericho. They devoutly hoped to be of assistance in breaking up the plot, for had not Ruth's father (Arthur Ford) been a respected and still-revered rabbi who stood well with the elders of the temple? Fear nonetheless clutched at their hearts, and they hoped to reach Jerusalem in time for the Passover, so that they might ferret out the secrets of those who would do away with the Master.

Now the Guides returned to the ministry of Jesus, writing:

When the hourglass was gradually running out of sand, the Master took his disciples with him into a quiet place and asked each to carry on for the Father after his own days among them had ceased to be. Timothy could not accept the premise that Jesus would soon be leaving them, and he wanted to swear a covenant among them that Jesus would never be captured as long as one of them remained alive to protect him.

"Timothy, Timothy," Jesus reasoned with him, "dost think that I would need to be seized unless my Father had assigned the time and the place for the captors? Surely thou knowest that through the power of my Father I could protect myself from enemies, were it not that I came among thee to preach and teach and then to give my physical life that others might carry on."

"But, Master, we know little that we will be able to use in convincing others after thy death that thou wert as a God among us if you are captured and put from us." This from Thomas.

And Jesus spake, "Yea, but after three days in the tomb I shall again walk among ye, and then shall thou know that God is indeed in charge of all that befalls even the least of these, our brothers."

Peter, agape, shouted, "Master, do we understand that thou shalt return to life even as Lazarus did? Then why are we worrying? Lazarus is as vigorous and brilliant as before he lay in the tomb, so if thou shalt let them snuff the life from thee, only to return in three days, we can indeed taunt the unbelievers with their evil and willful ways."

Jesus smiled at Peter's exuberance, but shook his head, saying, "That is not quite the way it shall be, Peter." And as he and others burst forth with more questions, Jesus held up a hand, saying, "Ye shall see what ye shall see when the time is at hand, but until then abide with me, and we will spread the good word of God's yearning for all His children."

Once again I wished that there were some verification for incidents such as this, of which the Gospels make no mention. But whenever I challenged the Guides, they would imperturbably reply, "What we are telling you is the truth."

Now we return to the closing days of the ministry of the Son of God, called Jesus. Knowing that his time in physical body was drawing toward its close, Jesus took some of his disciples with him and returned to Nazareth, where he told his mother, Mary, that she was not to lament when his time came, for he had been born to die that others might live, and the manner of his passing had been decreed since before he entered the flesh.

Grief flooded the heart of Mary at his words. Yet an exultation seized her simultaneously, knowing that she had given birth to a man who was beyond all others in his faith and purity of spirit. She asked if she might accompany him to Jerusalem for the Passover, and after some hesitation he replied that she would be welcome as far as the house of Lazarus, after which his own final days and hours were ordained to be spent in the company of those disciples who would carry on the mission of the Father. Together they paid a last visit to the Sea of Galilee, where Jesus spoke to untold multitudes and expressed the hope that no sacrifice would be too great for them when the time came to attest to their faith and love of God.

Then they turned southward along the Jordan heights, avoiding those areas where Jesus might have been seized before his final mission was completed. At the house of Lazarus they received the message from Ruth and Jonathan, thanking Jesus for his revival of her beloved brother. And before Jesus at last bade his mother farewell, their message also came warning of the plot they had learned about in Mesopotamia.

"So be it," Jesus replied while the others expressed consternation at the evil tidings.

"But, Master," Mary said, kneeling at his feet, "we would hide thee any place that brother Lazarus or you feels is secure. Do not risk thy dear presence in Jerusalem at this time."

With a gentle smile, Jesus touched the hair of the kneeling woman and rejoined, "Nay, it is written, and what will be will be."

"But, Master, surely it is unwise to walk boldly into a trap that has been laid for thee," Martha protested. But Jesus exchanged understanding glances with Lazarus, saying, "Where is the hole so deep that a man may hide and still preserve his self-respect? Thus it is with those who would bury their light so deeply that it would no longer serve as a beacon for those to follow." Continuing, Jesus said: "Lazarus, my brother, preserve this haven for all those who hunger for the truth and yearn for the light so that it will be as a shrine to that which you and I have always known. Protect our dear sisters here, and let their light shine forth on all who arrive without lanterns, thirsting for truth. I go now to prepare a place for thee and thy loved ones, and for all those who cherish the true God and perform His works. Believe on me."

To each he gave a tender embrace, knowing full well that he was embarking on the final week of his physical being.

It was Palm Sunday as you celebrate it today when Jesus had his greatest triumph, entering Jerusalem on a donkey with palms strewn in his path by admiring citizenry. It also marked the last time of such triumph, for within a week he was to be scourged and abused as few men have ever been. He was a human man in whom dwelt the Christ Spirit. Thus he suffered even as you or I would, but because of his indwelling knowledge he also saw the purpose behind it all.

Reverting to the parallel story of Ruth, the Guides then addressed me directly, writing:

On this sacred date (Palm Sunday) you and Jonathan were in Capernaum, and you walked with some of the followers along the shores of Galilee, yearning to spare Jesus the harm that had been foretold to you in Mesopotamia. But the forces were gathering, and there was naught that anyone could do to spare him the final physical ordeal. In fact, the adulation of the crowds heightened the decision of the high priests to rid themselves of this threat to their supreme power with the Jewish people, and that day the die was cast.

Skipping four days, they wrote:

On the eve of the Passover, after visiting the temple, Jesus and his disciples went straightaway to the roof of the house he had earlier indicated to them as a place for their sacrament with him, and there they observed the feast of the Passover. When he did break his bread, he passed a morsel down the table to each of the others, saying, "Eat this in remembrance of me." And when he had tasted his wine, he sent the glass around the table, saying, "Each of ye drink this in remembrance of me."

"But, Master," John asked, "why in 'remembrance' of thee when thou art here among us, and wholly unforgettable?"

The Guides then recounted the beautiful story of that Last

Supper, but since the conversation between Jesus and the disciples was put into direct quotes, and there were numerous exchanges among Judas Iscariot, Peter, and Jesus, I have chosen to omit this segment because, lacking proof, I do not wish to intrude on such a sacred ceremony. The Guides then switched back to Ruth, writing:

On that same eve of the Passover Ruth and Jonathan were still far away, for they had been delayed in Capernaum, and that night Ruth had a dream in which she saw the crumpled body of Jesus laid into a tomb, from which he then arose in a blaze of light, an aura surrounding his head and angels descending from heaven to sing hallelujahs. She awakened with a start, and so real was the dream that she woke Jonathan to tell him of her fears. Jonathan reassured her, saying the dream was likely caused by the news that her brother Lazarus had been raised from the tomb, but she would not be appeased. "If only," she sighed, "we had not been delayed and could have reached Jerusalem before the Passover."

"Fear not," Jonathan said, "we will be there within a few days and then all will be well, for we will enlist help in protecting the Master, so that no harm will befall him."

The Guides, after completing their account of the Last Supper, then resumed their narrative:

Jesus led his small group of disciples to the Mount of Olives, where they stretched out under the olive trees in Gethsemane to rest and watch the torchlights across the Kedron Valley in the holy city of Jerusalem. Jesus asked his disciples to watch with him and then went apart to pray, seeking strength to withstand the coming ordeal. When he returned to his little band of followers, he found all asleep. Waking Peter and John, he asked, "Could thee not watch with me this hour?"

"Master, forgive me," Peter said, "but a strange lassitude

vercame me, and against my very will I seemed put to
leep."

"Yea," John said, "it was as if I were drugged, Master,
or one moment I was wide awake and in the next I slept
like the dead. See, the others sleep heavily, without tossing
or seeming to hear our voices. Could it be, Master, that
omething was added to our food or wine?"

"Alibis!" Jesus replied with a teasing smile. And then
e added more seriously, "Perhaps it is the peace of our
ather which has descended on thee, to prepare thee for
he test that lies ahead."

"What test is that, Lord?" Peter asked. "Surely we have
vercome every hurdle, and thy followers are even now
arrying thy message far and wide. Where is Judas Iscariot?
We are all here except him."

A sigh escaped the lips of Jesus as he replied, "He is
ow on his way here to do that which he is about to do."

"And what is that, Lord?" John asked. Then in the dis-
ince they heard the thud of many feet, and suddenly
udas ran through the trees shouting, "Here he is." Ignor-
ig his fellow disciples, he embraced Jesus and would have
issed him, but at the all-wise and knowing look the Master
ave him he shrank to one side. Then men burst forth
rom the trees to seize the son of man.

"What goes here?" shouted Bartholemew, who had been
wakened with the others by the sound of heavy footsteps.
As the men laid hand on Jesus to manacle him, Peter drew
is sword and struck at the leader, but the man stepped
uickly aside and the knife severed the ear of a servant.

"Nay, Peter," Jesus said, "we are come to heal and not
) wound." With that he replaced the ear, which adhered
nd promptly became as the other one. The servant, ten-
erly feeling the ear that only a moment before had lain
n the ground, fell to his knees in wonderment. But the
thers, many of whom had not seen the incident, blocked
ff the Master from his disciples, and at sword point began

marching him out of the garden and down the hill t
the Kedron Valley.

Some of the disciples fled for cover, thinking they to
would be arrested; but Peter and John, who were neare
to the Master, slipped from tree to tree in the shadow
of the night, until they could begin to follow after th
soldiers in a roundabout manner, keeping them in sigl
to discover their destination.

*Familiar as I am with the Biblical story of Jesus' last da
and hours, I was eager to read the continuing account by tl
Guides. But like modern-day writers of suspense novels, they no
skipped to the alleged daughter of Arthur Ford and her husban
writing:*

Now let us return to Ruth and Jonathan, who were rusl
ing homeward from Capernaum. Strange foreboding
obsessed Ruth, and although Jonathan tried to reassu
her, it was for naught. Within herself she sensed calamit
and the dream continued to trouble her, for had not Jes
himself indicated that his life in physical body would so
be drawing to a close? At one night's stop with a carava
they heard a strange tale of a man being seized an
executed, and although some said it was a robber, anoth
insisted that it was a good and holy man who hung c
a cross outside the city gates of Jerusalem. They anxious
pressed onward toward the house of Lazarus, who wou
surely know what was happening. But one of the donke
was so tired he refused to be prodded, and thus they d
not reach Bethany until midmorning of the day after tl
Jewish Sabbath.

It was a devastating homecoming, for there they learne
from Martha and Lazarus that Jesus had been put to dea
on a cross, and he was then lying in a tomb provid
by their friend Joseph of Arimathea. At word of this cata

ophe they fell on their knees and prayed to God that
ll was well with His son whom they loved more than their
wn lives, and the two men also wept.

"Where is Mary?" Ruth finally asked, aware of how
eenly her sister would feel the loss, and Martha said early
nat morning she had gone, together with Mary of Magdala
nd the mother of Jesus to Golgotha that they might kneel
here and pray for their beloved Jesus. Ruth and Jonathan,
xhausted from the tiring and hurried journey, finally fell
sleep after the midday meal, but in a short while were
wakened by excited voices and the exclamations of
azarus.

Pulling on robes, they hastened to the loggia, where
lary Magdalene, throwing herself into Ruth's arms, ex-
laimed, "Ruth, Ruth, I have seen him. Jesus lives!"

"Then it was another who was crucified!" Jonathan
xclaimed in vast relief.

"No, no," Mary the sister of Lazarus gasped. "He was
ndeed crucified, for the other two Marys saw him and
poke to him while he was on the cross."

"Then someone rescued him before it was too late?"
onathan asked. And Mary replied, "Alas, no. He was dead,
or they ran a spear into his side, but then he was taken
lown and our friend Joseph asked permission to tend
is body and lay him in his own unused tomb."

"Yes? Yes?" Ruth prompted quickly. And Mary of Mag-
lala replied, "Early this morning we went near his tomb
o pray, and I decided to go still nearer it, even though
entries were stationed there. I crept forward, wanting
o assure myself that his grave had not been desecrated
luring the night, and lo, the sentries were sleeping and
he stone had been rolled aside. In a panic I rushed toward
he tomb, but from a glance inside I could see that it was
mpty. Then a man appeared before me, and thinking
hat he was a gardener, I pleaded, 'If thou hast taken

away his body, please tell me where thou hast laid him.'

Here Mary of Magdala broke into loud sobs and th
others looked questioningly at the other two Marys, bu
Mary Magdalene recovered quickly, and with shining eye
exclaimed, "It was he! It was our Lord Jesus and he spok
to me, saying, 'Mary, knowest me not?' "

"Incredible," Jonathan muttered under his breath. Bu
Mary Magdalene continued excitedly, "I tell thee that wha
I am speaking is the truth. I threw myself at his feet anc
would have kissed his robe except that he told me no
to touch him, for he had not yet ascended to his Father.

Mystified, Jonathan asked how such a thing could b
true, and he so strongly indicated by his tone that h
thought Mary was imagining that Lazarus spoke for th
first time, saying, "If he were able to restore physical lif
to such as me, do you doubt, Jonathan, that he could d
it for himself?"

Then Jonathan was ashamed, for in the excitement h
had temporarily forgotten the message they had receive
that Lazarus was raised from the tomb by Jesus durin
their absence.

Ruth, exalted with the wonder of all they had heard
embraced her younger brother Lazarus in her arms, saying
"God be praised, for we have indeed been privileged t
walk and talk with His holy son." And Mary the, mothe
of Jesus, a beatific smile on her face, knelt with them whil
they held a prayer service of thanksgiving.

Then they heard joyful shouts, and Peter and John cam
rushing into the house, shouting, "He is risen! The Maste
is risen! We have seen him, and the tomb is bare of a
except his grave clothes."

"So Mary has told us," Lazarus said, his face alight wit
rapture. "Think thee that he will be coming here this day?

"I know not," Peter said, "except that he told us he woul
see us again in Galilee."

"Ah, his beloved Galilee," Mary the mother of Jesus said softly. "Then let us return to our homes there and await his coming." And she went to prepare for her departure with John, to whose care she had been entrusted.

The Guides now returned to the events that had transpired during the period from the fateful Thursday evening when Jesus was seized until the close of the first Good Friday. They related in great detail how Jesus was taken first to the Sanhedrin, where Peter uttered his fearful denials; then of the appearances before Pontius Pilate and Herod, and finally of his crucifixion at Golgotha. Since their account coincides closely with that of the Gospels, I am omitting the familiar story. But of what transpired after the crucifixion, the Guides wrote:

The earthquake that day was a natural occurrence, but the guilty conscience of the priests and the people impressed it vigorously on their memory. The disciples were awed, and before the day ended they were not only griefstricken but terrorized. When Joseph of Arimathea sought permission to claim the body of Christ, it was readily given, for the authorities were afraid that it was the magical power of Jesus that had brought on the earth tremors. Thus the body was anointed, wrapped in linen, and laid to rest, with a stone before the opening.

On that first Easter morning Jesus came forth from the tomb to prove that life is everlasting. Angels or guardian spirits had removed the stone, only so that followers would quickly discover the fact, because his spirit did not require an open door to leave the tomb. Now that Jesus was spirit, the physical body was cast off and became molecules rearranged to form different patterns, and the followers would not again see the physical body, although they saw Jesus several times in his spiritual form, which was made manifest to resemble the physical body. Thus he demon-

strated the indestructibility of matter as well as spirit, fo
the body became simple elements again when the ma
Jesus became the resurrected Jesus, or Christ spirit.

I am, of course, familiar with the phenomenon that is call
materialization. But what the Guides seem to indicate here
that because of his special relationship with God, Jesus can ma
himself visible whenever he chooses through supernatural power
Certainly he has no need for the darkened séance chamber, wi
its dim red bulb, which psychics employ in their alleged materializ
tions of the deceased by means of ectoplasm.

10

Day of Pentecost

Possibly, I thought, the Guides would now wind up their story with a brief summation and hopefully comment on what finally became of Arthur Ford's alleged daughter, Ruth. But they move in their own mysterious ways, and the next morning, as if there had been no interruption, they began:

Now to go back to the house of Lazarus. By ones and twos came the disciples and other close followers, and their hearts were heavy despite the reports that Christ had risen. Would they ever see the Master again? At their prompting, Lazarus retold the circumstances of his own return from the dead, and since all could see that he was healthy and solid in flesh, they began to take heart and gradually to separate. But it was agreed that after some had tended to urgent business, they would make their way to the Sea of Galilee.

John escorted the mother Mary, who was returning directly to Capernaum, and the others went separate ways. But the day came when the disciples who were fishermen recognized Jesus near a lonely stretch of the Galilean shore, and he supped with them. Some had seen him before, or thought they had, when he suddenly appeared to them within a locked room. Hope soared in their breasts, but still they wondered how they would be able to carry on the work that he had bade them do, without their super-natural·leader.

A rally was to be held on the day of Pentecost, and at that time the Holy Spirit descended on the disciples with such force that all were fired with wisdom and power. A multitude had gathered, and as each disciple spoke in his own tongue, all others were able to comprehend as if it had been uttered in their own dialects and languages. This has no connection with glossolalia, as it is called in Pentecostal churches today, for none is able to comprehend these strange mouthings; but on the day of Pentecost each heard the inspired words in his own tongue. Thus it was comprehensible to all, and they fell on their knees to give thanks that such power was available in that sin-bespotted land.

I was interested to note their reference to glossolalia, because in recent years I have read of the rapidly growing Pentecostal movement and of the services during which members of the audience speak in unrecognizable tongues that seem nevertheless to have the structure of languages. But I often wondered why this phenomenon has been compared to the day of Pentecost, since the New Testament states that on that occasion all understood the words, whereas today no one comprehends glossolalia. Perhaps sensing my confusion, the Guides declared:

Let us explain in more detail. After the appearance in Galilee and several other places Jesus gathered himself more closely into the realm of his Father; and feeling that his work in flesh was finished, he then departed from the ken of his followers, although he is always able to show himself at any needed time.

At the day of Pentecost he sent the gift of tongues to the apostles, and although many were baffled because the meaning was being understood in any language, those closest to Jesus while in flesh accepted it as simply another manifestation of his ability to perform acts of God that men call miracles. On that memorable day all the disciples and many hundreds of followers had assembled at a knoll not far from Bethany and Jerusalem.

The reference to "all the disciples" brought Judas to mind, and at a later time I asked what had become of him. The Guides wrote: "That unhappy, misguided man, when he heard what had happened to Jesus, rushed to fling the dirty coin into the faces of those who had bribed him. Then he ran into the countryside, and seeing a limb overhanging the roadway, he tore his cloak into segments, tied the strips together, and after looping one end around his neck, made a sort of lasso. Scaling the lower part of the tree, he then suspended the other end of the cloth rope from the limb and jumped from it, breaking his neck and hanging there until he passed from body, there to torture himself for eons on the other side we term the spirit plane. Judas has not reincarnated and is trying on this side to make amends, although the way is long and dark because of the knowledge within his own soul that he committed the blackest of sins. Yet remember that had he not done so, another means would have been found to end the physical life of Jesus, for his work in that form had already achieved the miracle of eternal life. There are no accidents."

Returning to the day of Pentecost, the Guides continued:

Peter led off the services, and although there were those gathered from as far away as Persia, Egypt, and today's Sudan, the inspired words that poured from his lips were heard by each in his own language. At first Peter was unaware of this, for since he spoke only Aramaic he assumed that others present would translate what he had said.

Remember that Peter himself scarcely knew what he was saying until the words poured forth, for he had simply begun to speak of the discipleship and of how Jesus had transformed their simple working lives into a state of daily walking with God. But as he began to speak, new thoughts seemed to fill him with a sort of ecstasy, and he spoke as a man bewitched. Then it was the turn of James and Andrew, and the same mystical power seized each of them by turn, until all who stood in the huge throng were dumbfounded and began whispering one to another, "Where or from whence has this astounding depth of knowledge filled these simple fishermen? How is it that they speak perfectly in so many foreign tongues that we are filled to overflowing with the impact of their message?"

Others began to speak, and among them was Jonathan who first told of his aversion to the very sound of Jesus' name, and then of his conversion when he at last saw and met the Savior. As Jonathan spoke, each understood in his native tongue, and Ruth, who knew so many languages, seemed to hear the inspired words in every language simultaneously.

Ruth apparently did not receive this power of tongues, because at another point the Guides remarked that she "listened in awe" to her husband's message. Ah, well, it was very much a man's world in Israel, and I do not recall any account in the four Gospels of a woman being permitted to address the throngs who followed Jesus.

It was an astonishing performance, and the disciples were no less astounded than the masses who heard simple fishermen speak with such erudition and power. Before the services ended, hundreds of new followers had been converted, and the word spread that although Jesus had been crucified, yet did he live and walk among men, although nonbelievers saw him not. Thus was the word carried to every fringe of the subcontinent, and although Stephen, a beloved convert, gave his life to be stoned to death, yet did new converts appear and swell the growing tide of converted souls who were ready to lay down their lives for the man whom some had never seen or heard or known.

Ruth and Jonathan agreed that day to set forth shortly to Greece and Macedonia to spread the word of the Master's rebirth, and the disciples drew lots to see which areas should receive their messages of love and brotherhood.

Lazarus had not gone to the meeting on that day of Pentecost, for again he had become afflicted with the fevers, and the two younger sisters had remained to nurse him. The fevers left him at the time of Pentecost, but his spirit seemed unwilling to linger long in physical frame, and when Ruth and Jonathan stopped off to see him, they were grieved at his seeming listlessness without physical cause.

When all were together in the loggia, Lazarus spoke thusly: "Dearly beloved ones, find it in thy hearts to forgive me, for I am weary of this world and eager to follow our beloved friend Jesus. We all are aware that our own father, Jeremiah [Arthur Ford], also awaits in the spirit, and I would join him there. His property, that I have administered for you since his passing, will be divided equally among the three of you, my adored sisters, and Mary and Martha will continue to live in this house as long as they choose. But the larger portion that has been amassed since our father's passing shall go to the disciples, to further the work of our lord Jesus and that in which all of us so firmly believe."

"No, no," Ruth said, "give also to the disciples' work, that portion of our father Jeremiah's estate that is mine as well, for I have no need of it, and Peter, John, Andrew, and the others can use it well to spread the truth about Jesus far beyond the confines of our troubled land."

"So be it." Lazarus smiled.

11

Lazarus– The Second Passing

The Guides showed no indication of slackening their pace, but since Jesus had now departed his physical body, I had no wish to be taken through the entire book of Acts at this time. I therefore asked if they would confine their dictation to parallel information that was not recorded in the New Testament. They seemed to be agreeable to that suggestion, because they wrote responsively:

After Pentecost the disciples and followers scattered around Palestine and the Middle East, spreading the word and even welcoming a few Gentiles to the sect that was beginning to be called Christian. Ruth and Jonathan went first to Greece, where they talked with Jews and Gentiles, explaining the teachings to the best of their ability and instructing them in the way of Christ: Love one another. Do good to those who hurt you. Share with others, and feel such love in thy heart that hatred will never again exist on this earth.

Some were enthusiastic, while others scoffed at such revolutionary heresy, for were we not meant to keep that which we earned by the sweat of our brow? Why help others who were too lazy to work or too incapable of earning a good living? Some would go to heaven and others to hell, so why interfere? Yet gradually the teaching spread, and while they were stopping in various ports to see con--

verts already chosen by some of the disciples to work with them, Ruth and Jonathan heard an exciting story about a man called Saul of Tarsus, who had seen Jesus in a great light on the road to Damascus and had later been healed of the blindness that came upon him at that time.

Now Saul, who was now called Paul, was not only a believer but also a teacher of the word, and those who knew of his conversion said that until that moment he had been a persecutor of Christians, so that the dramatic quality of his reversal served to draw others to the way of the cross. Paul had retired to his home to ponder that which had befallen him, and thence went Ruth and Jonathan to call on this small but mighty man.

They saw him from afar and knew him by the strange light that seemed to emanate from his person. When they told him of their association with Jesus and of Ruth's friendship with him since early childhood, he was enraptured and questioned them at length, asking about the revival of Lazarus from the tomb and the wondrous things they had witnessed at first hand.

"If only I had known him then!" Paul kept repeating. "Ah, but I know him now in such light that to the end of my days I shall do naught but serve him, how I do not yet know."

"By telling your story," Ruth replied softly. "Surely none but thee has such a tale to tell of the continuing life and power of the man from Nazareth."

"Yes," Jonathan agreed, "even we who knew and served him while he was in the flesh have no such dramatic witness to give as thee, for thou wert smitten by a man whom the world calls dead, and thou knowest that he lives."

"I am a Roman," Paul replied, "yet never have I doubted that that which happened to me is beyond the realm of the law. Within the kingdom of God are more wondrous occurrences than Caesar could ever dream of. I will dedicate my life to spreading the good news that man lives on, not just in the bosom of Abraham as we Jews are wont to think, but in the very heart of Jehovah our God. Devious are the ways of the politicians, but straight is the path of the Lord, and from this day forward will I follow that rigid path, though it take me through temptation, starvation, or the pitfalls of hades, for I am cleansed in the way of the Lord and He will be my Redeemer."

Fantastic, I mused, how the Palestinian Ruth got around in those days. Not only did she know Jesus and the disciples, according to the Guides, but now Paul as well. Remote as the possibility seems, if I did indeed have any connection with that other Ruth, perhaps it was from her that I inherited my wanderlust, for I too have traveled often and far. But whereas I was interviewing ambassadors and heads of state, she was associating with the most immortal band of men the Christian world has ever known. How I envied her!

Ruth and Jonathan spent several days at the home of Paul before beginning their homeward journey. At Capernaum they stopped to see the mother-in-law of Peter, who was bustling as ever about the simple cottage and singing the praises of him who saved her from the fevers of death. James and Andrew were there, bringing reports of their work and the numbers of conversions; but Peter was busy with affairs of the movement in Jerusalem, and the disciples spoke glowingly of his powerful work and the message that he brought to those who would heed it.

A few followers had been stoned to death, and Ruth was anxious about her family in Bethany, until assured of their safety. The disciples were careful to go about their work in such manner that they would not arouse the open opposition of the priests, and had not thus far been molested.

Some followers who were carried away by the zeal to

convert all in an instant gave less heed to the proprieties
and thus became victims of the mob. Stephen they lamented
still, but where each had fallen, a dozen sprang up to take
his place, and the movement was spreading. Ruth and
Jonathan told about their visit to Paul, and although some
had felt his seeming conversion was a ruse to prosecute
from within, those who heard their story were convinced
of its reality, and word was carried to Peter in Jerusalem
that Paul of Tarsus was indeed one of them.

The mother of Jesus, who was then in Capernaum, sat
with them during some of the discussions, and her heart
lightened as she heard proof that her son still lived, with
power beyond the conception of mankind. A young man
named Luke, an ardent convert of Paul's who had once
met Jesus briefly, came one day; and it was then Mary
divulged to the little group the deep secret that had long
lain within her heart, telling of the visitation from the
angels and of the strange manner in which she conceived
and bore Jesus.

Ruth listened in awe, for although she vividly remembered the star and the visit from the Magi, she was unaware
that the birth had long been heralded and a child conceived,
not by man, but by the Father in heaven.

"It was a difficult cross for my beloved husband, Joseph,"
Mary said softly, "but he too was told in a dream that
no other man had known me and that he had been chosen
to father the child who would revolutionize the thinking
of the world. To the world Joseph gave the appearance
of the physical father, but what we two knew of the truth
lay heavy in our hearts, for always there was a shadow,
knowing that the beloved son would be slaughtered like
an innocent lamb. Joseph gave up his life before that dread-
ful event at Golgotha, but as surely as if he had lived
through it he saw the road that lay ahead for the son
of his heart. Now both of them are gone from my sight,
but they live in my heart; and I have other children of
Joseph's who are doubly dear to me because of their stead-

fast love and devotion to their older brother, Jesus. The Lord be praised!"

On reading these words, I was again disturbed by the Guides' habit of directly quoting these sacred characters of the Bible. I have absolutely no proof of the veracity of these events. But at this point I consulted the Encyclopaedia Britannica *and read that Luke, "the beloved physician," was indeed a convert of Paul's and is considered to be the author of Acts as well as the gospel called Luke. Turning again to the New Testament, I learned that the book of Luke gives the only full account of the miraculous conception of Jesus, and Mark and John do not even mention it.*

I can only conclude that either the Guides know whereof they speak or Arthur Ford, since passing on, has retained a remarkable memory for the contents of the Bible. After all, he was a Christian minister in his last life.

On the morning that Ruth and Jonathan departed from Capernaum a large crowd gathered outside the tabernacle to see these faithful followers of Jesus, and Ruth was pleased that not only James and Andrew but also Jonathan responded with quiet dignity to the questions hurled at them by doubters and nonbelievers. To those who truly sought information they spoke with fervor, and their eyes shone with adoration as they discussed their friendship with him who had gone on to prepare a place for all men, that all might live and none need die.

"How is it that at the day of Pentecost you fishermen spoke so that all might understand, each in his own tongue?" asked one aged Jew who had seen that miracle manifested. "Yet now you answer only in Aramaic and need Ruth as an interpreter."

"We understand it not ourselves," Andrew replied, "except that on that memorable day the power of God poured into and through us, and we spake as never before. Now once again we are imprisoned with our own dialect and native tongue, yet the fire burns with equal ardor within us, and the Lord speaks through us."

According to the Guides, then, the disciples lost their ability to speak in tongues after that one occasion; and although I am not a student of the Bible, I recall no incident in which that miraculous talent was again referred to.

Then Ruth and Jonathan began the final leg of their journey, and they went directly to Bethany, where Mary and Martha anxiously awaited them. As soon as they came within hailing distance, the sisters began running toward them, breathlessly saying that Jesus had been there with Lazarus for a brief time, talking earnestly. But when they approached him with a cry of welcome, he disappeared from their presence, and Lazarus had viewed the two sisters reproachfully, reminding them that this was no ordinary visit and they would have been well advised to await a personal summons. Now Lazarus was ailing again, and although they were ministering to him with love and solicitude, he seemed to have lost the zest for living and was failing before their eyes.

Ruth and Jonathan went hurriedly to see Lazarus, who was lying on a low couch. He greeted them with a thin smile, saying, "I have been awaiting only your return, so that all affairs might be adjusted properly before I take my departure."

Ruth knew instantly that he spoke of withdrawal from the physical body, but she pretended to think that he referred to a trip and asked where he might be going.

"To rejoin our dearly beloved Jesus in the kingdom of our Father," he replied quietly. "I have served out my time in the flesh and will not be returning, dear Ruth and Jonathan. But heed well what Jesus spake to me while he was here within the last few days. 'Thou wilt serve with me in paradise,' he said unto me, 'and the others will serve yet a little longer in the vineyard of the Lord, for there is work to be done, and those dearly beloved sisters of thine will seek to do that which our heavenly Father requires of them before their task is finished. Say unto Jonathan, "Feed my sheep." And to his spouse, Ruth, say, "Be thou ever alert to serve others as well as to sense their needs." To Martha I say, "Continue in thy good works, caring for the needs of those who pass this way for solace and sustenance." And to Mary I say, "Remember all that which I have told thee in our talks, and to others give of thy sweet self in loving attention." . . .'

"Thus I go, dear ones," Lazarus continued, looking around the circle at the four who were so near and dear to him, "and be assured that thou art ever in my heart throughout eternity, even as God enfolds us in His bosom."

Jonathan took his hand and kissed it, and the sisters knelt while the spirit of Lazarus once again passed from his physical body.

After a brief pause Arthur Ford apparently took over the dictation, and I sensed the different pressure on the typing keys as he wrote: "In connection with that visit of Jesus to my son Lazarus I would explain thusly. Lazarus, who was so like a brother unto him, recognized instantly that Jesus was not of the flesh, but had shown himself in spiritual body like unto his physical one.

"Lazarus, who had once been in spirit form with me, was not surprised in the least, and spoke with the Master as naturally as if both were in the same medium. Although Jesus appeared solid to Mary and Martha, Lazarus differentiated and realized that he would soon be joining him in the spirit plane. Thus he prepared to lay down the cross of physical life and ready himself for the great adventure he would soon be commencing."

The Guides gave no further glimpse, then or ever, of the life that Lazarus continued after death.

CHAPTER

12

Deaths of Jonathan and Ruth

*D*uring my travels in the Holy Land *more than a decade ago, I learned that many of the sacred sites now revered as the birthplaces and tombs of Jesus and other Biblical characters were designated as such by the mother of Constantine the Great some three hundred years later. Thus, controversy continues to this day about the authenticity of some of these traditional sites.*

Before beginning the next session, I therefore asked if the tomb shown to me in Bethany was actually that from which Jesus called forth Lazarus, and the Guides wrote: "The tomb was approximately in that location, and near that of his father, Jeremiah [Arthur Ford], and mother, Sarah. Since the disposal of a body is of little import on this side, the exact location is not definite."

I asked if the traditional tomb of Jesus, now within the walls of a vast cathedral in Jerusalem, was the one actually occupied briefly by the Master, and they replied, "Hardly the same." Then I wanted to know about his birthplace beneath that other great church in Bethlehem, and the Guides responded: "The area is now so paved by the church that who could truly say which cave beneath the inn was then so occupied? All of this is of little import. It is the worshipful feeling that persists, and the love of God and his son Jesus that counts. The where *is not important. It is the* why *and the* how *that matter." They then resumed the narrative.*

When Lazarus was again laid tenderly in the tomb from

which Jesus had once called him forth, Ruth remained for a few days with Mary and Martha, while Jonathan proceeded to their home in Jericho. The sisters deliberated at length about the best course for the two unmarried ones to follow, and eventually they decided that, as Lazarus had suggested, they should remain at the house in Bethany to provide succor for those who were weary and heavy-laden.

Word then went forth to the disciples that they were always welcome at the houses of Lazarus and Jonathan, and as the followers grew in numbers, they stopped often at the two houses for renewal of spirit as well as physical body. Often were the times that Peter, John, and the others came for long evenings of talk, rest, and relaxation.

As the movement waxed in force, the authorities in Jerusalem eyed it with alarm, and especially did they protest the statements of those who claimed to have seen Jesus since the Resurrection. Because the unwed sisters of Lazarus were among those who had seen the Lord after his death on the cross, agents of the Sanhedrin kept a watchful eye on their house, but never once did they find reason for interference, since the two women lived quietly except for the coming and going of many guests. Thus the days passed uneventfully.

Then one day a brother of the Lord Jesus, while visiting in Bethany, told them that Paul of Tarsus had asked permission to see the tomb where Lazarus was laid to rest. At first Martha and Mary were fearful that in some way it might be disturbed, for they remembered the persecutions that Paul (or Saul) had launched against the followers of Jesus after his death. But James the brother of Jesus reassured them, saying that never was a man more changed than Paul after his conversion in a great light, and they gave their consent. Paul came, and immediately they liked him, for he was not only a bear of a man but also a warm and humorous one when not seized by the zeal of his ministry.

After a time they led him to the tomb, and Paul dropped to his knees, head almost touching the earth as he prayed to the Father that he might someday have the privilege of seeing and knowing Jesus and Lazarus in the land beyond the grave. The fragrance of mimosa filled the air beside the tomb, and the sisters looked wonderingly one at the other, because none grew in that area.

When Paul finished his prayers, he arose, and looking toward the heavens, raised his arms in a great cry of yearning for God's word, and all seemed to hear spoken softly the words, "I am here." A hush fell on the little group; then the words came again, "Here I am." The spell of it held them in its embrace, and although they saw naught, they felt the presence of him who had once raised Lazarus from the tomb. Thus they were made glad with his presence and were glorified with the knowledge that for those who follow in his way there is no death, but sleeping.

This called to mind Arthur Ford's assertion in A World Beyond *that most souls sleep for a time after "passing through the open door called death." He said those on the "other side" do not disturb them until they themselves are ready to awaken, but when that time comes there are many to assist them in making the adjustment and getting on about the business of living.*

As the writing resumed, the Guides addressed me directly, declaring:

In the Palestine that Jesus knew were many caravans that took the great trade routes from Egypt through the fertile crescent to Iran, as we call Persia today. When you and Jonathan set out on one of your journeys after the Pentecost you traveled that route, and while in Persia studied under a sage known as Belthezar. He was learned in astronomy and astrology, and when the stars shone from their heavenly thrones, he pointed out to you a comet that would return again and again in flaming sparks to lead the way. This was to you a miracle of God's word, and as you watched it flaming across the evening skies, you knelt in prayer to ask that so long as you should live, you wished to serve God also as a flaming torch to light the way for others.

This, then, has returned with you each time that you took new physical form: this aching desire to serve God, even as you have failed often in that quest for perfection and holiness. Let this story serve again as a beacon for you, and try to match the fiery torch of the heavens that lights the way for others, forgetting *self* in the flash and brilliance of the comet's progress across the heavens, dwelling only upon the light that shines forth to deliver the message of God's all-seeing, all-knowing Being.

These words at first struck me as fanciful and high-flown. Here was I, a nobody, being told that before birth I had pledged myself to help others find the way to serve God. I remembered that from earliest childhood memory I had wanted to be a foreign missionary, but in my teens I decided to be a newspaper reporter instead. When that opportunity came, I devoted my life to the printed word, writing the day-to-day news of the world, which was seldom inspirational. But as I continued to muse about the Guides' words, I wondered if perhaps karma had indeed directed the course of my life. The Guides have stressed that there are "few accidents in this world," and after my chance meeting with Arthur Ford and the subsequent development of automatic writing, I became so influenced by Lily's inspirational writings that, against the wishes of my family, I published A Search for the Truth.

Eventually I gave up my syndicated political column to devote full time to writing other psychic books, and since then I have received many thousands of letters from unknown readers who say that reading the books has changed their lives, prevented them from committing suicide, or led them back to God.

It is an eerie feeling to discover that we, who think we control our own destiny, are actually a small but integral part of a cosmic plan, and that our destiny may already have been determined before we entered physical body. I am anything but a zealot, yet perhaps a "still, small voice within" directed me to become a well-known newspaper writer in order that those who, accustomed to recognizing truth when reading my daily by-line, could more easily accept that which the Guides have written through me. As the Spanish say, "Quién sabe?"

To return to the Guides:

During the remaining years together you and Jonathan traveled to many places in the ancient world. For a time you spread the gospel in Greece and Macedonia, and there you again saw Paul and met many of his early followers. Although you and Jonathan were Jews, as was Paul, you worked frequently among the Gentiles, who were eager to hear of this strange and powerful God who could restore life to the dead. Because you were a sister of Lazarus, they asked again and again for the details of his return from the dead. Jonathan frequently told the story of his own bitter hatred for the teachings of Jesus and of his conversion after the Master insisted that you return home to your family.

Many were the times that you and Jonathan had to leave a meeting hurriedly and slip from the city in the dark of night, for the Jews were mainly against this teaching. Some of them converted to Christianity, but the more orthodox hated the very name "Jesus of Nazareth" and scourged those who would draw the people into the light of this new and wondrous way. For many years you traveled with Jonathan, and your daughters grew strong in the faith as they too began speaking to the youth of those lands.

Since this was the first mention of Ruth's two children in some time, I asked for more information about them, and the Guides surprised me by writing: "The daughter in Palestine who was then named Sarah, after your mother [Arthur Ford's wife], is now your sister, Margaret Overbeck. Sarita, as she was often called, was the younger of the two children, the one who became so faint from the desert heat and the glare of the sun that you had to return her to her father's house in Jericho. She was sweet and loving, giving of self to others and devoted to her father as well as to you and her older sister, who was named Esther for Jonathan's mother. Both girls were comely and animated, with a glow of love surrounding them; but as they grew older, it was Sarah who developed into the better speaker, as she addressed the youth in behalf of the man who was crucified that others might live. She was a great influence for good, then as now, thinking of others and gently assuming some of their burdens. Later in that life she was happily married to one of the younger followers of Christ's path, whose name was Jacob."

Arthur Ford then took over the typewriter, addressing me: "When the travels began after the death of my son Lazarus, you were ever eager to find new converts, and for this reason you had the aid of those on this side [of the door called death] who recognized the need for the journeys. Many were the perils in those times, and for a woman to travel so widely was not considered wise; but ever there were those here who served as guardians for you and others bent on spreading the 'good tidings of great joy.' For a long time there was dissension among the followers, many of whom had never seen Jesus. But the role of peacemaker was then strong within you, so why not again cultivate this trait, by bringing together those who are too ready to hear idle gossip and spread harmful tales? There is nothing new under the sun, as the Bible says, so use all talents previously developed, as you accumulate those others that need bringing into flower. Never step backward, but always ahead! How well this is recognized on this side, and now we pass along the message to you." The Group then continued:

In Syracuse were many who heeded the teachings, and because Mark and Luke were attractive younger men, steadfast in their faith, they had an impelling way of reaching those who might not otherwise have heeded the words of the impassioned Paul or Peter. The latter two were frequently at odds, but never for long because each walked in grace, and the Holy Spirit interceded to quench the fires of mistrust brought on by their clashing personalities. Once you were able to bring the two men together after a bitter quarrel about the tenets of their faith and the importance of bringing Gentiles into the brotherhood. This was in Ephesus, and thereafter it was generally agreed that Paul would concentrate his efforts principally on the uncircumcised, while Peter and the original disciples would mainly work among the Jews to bring them to the light.

Jonathan died of a heart attack after one of the meetings in Syria, when you were forced to leave hastily to avoid angry mobs of Jews, and his body was taken by you and others to Jericho, where it was buried. You then went to the house of Lazarus for a time, to be with your sisters. After that they sometimes traveled with you, but not on your longer trips to the newly established churches in the Tigris and Euphrates crescent, as they had many followers to care for at their home in Bethany.

Well, wait a minute! The Guides had neatly disposed of one of their "leading characters" in a single sentence, without emotion or drama, but I wanted to know how Ruth felt about Jonathan's death. To humor me, they replied: "It was the normal sadness of the one who is left behind. But Jonathan was so much older that it was not unexpected, and Ruth was rather practical, and also busy with her continuing work in the early Church."

"Why won't you tell me his identity?" I queried again. "Who was Jonathan?"

"Your present husband, Bob," they readily responded. "We did not want to tell you earlier, so that your subconscious would not color our writings through you." There was that Group Karma again! So Bob Montgomery was Jonathan, my Palestinian husband, and my sister Margaret was in that life our daughter Sarah.

If what the Guides say about karma is true, then the three of us must have pledged between lives to return in the present embodiment into circumstances where we would again find each other.

The Guides, after dropping those bombshells, smoothly resumed their narrative, writing:

Ever were you a friend of the mother Mary, and although she departed that life some years before your own departure, she was as a ministering angel to those who sought her out to hear from her holy lips the story of her son Jesus. She was ever helpful and full of zest, but when the time came for her to join the Father, she slipped so easily from her earthly body that none knew of it until many hours after, when her daughter and son-in-law found her sitting serenely in a sort of rocker that Joseph had made, a sweet smile on her lips, and her composure unmarred by any flutter of passage. It was as if an angel had kissed her on the brow and said, "Come, Mary, thy time has now arrived. Thou art needed with us from whence thou came."

Arthur Ford then concluded the Palestinian narrative with these words:

Fortunately for you, my daughter, you died before the destruction of Jerusalem and the surrounding countryside by Titus and Vespasian. It was a blessing to be spared that horror, for the suffering was intense and the inflamed spirits were put sorely to trial. Like your mother, you died of the fevers, and were buried peacefully beside Jonathan in Jericho.

Feeling a slight letdown, I asked, "When Ruth died, who was there to attend her services and to care?" Their reply:

"The church, the neighbors, and Mary and Martha, who survived you by a few years."

Epilogue

The story was ended, but some vexing questions remained. Why, for instance, did not Ruth or Jonathan, who appeared to be better educated than most of the disciples, leave a written record of Jesus' ministry? When I confronted the Guides with this puzzler, they replied:

"The idea did not occur to them, for not many were writing books in those days, and the time of Jesus was so filled with those people who knew at first hand or had heard witnesses to his good works that seemingly it would have been a thrice-told tale. Many there were who were jotting down accounts of his teachings and his miracles, but in the main they were not preserved in such manner as to reach the attention of church authorities two or three centuries later, when the New Testament was compiled.

"Many of these jottings were contained in letters or were simply notes for remembrance, and some of these precious accounts were written by certain disciples including James, the brother of Jesus. These writers were not thinking of their own fame, but were rather telling the story to those who had not yet heard the Word. Mark had access to some of this material, as did others who had known Peter and the original disciples.

"The book of John is the only Gospel partially written by an original disciple, and he wrote it in his old age, on realizing that those who had been eyewitnesses to the events were dying out, and a new generation would find it hard to carry on without the written word."

Recalling how unexpectedly the Dead Sea scrolls had been unearthed, to enrich our present store of knowledge about Biblical lore, I hopefully asked if Jesus himself wrote any messages or letters that will yet be found. Their reply: "None that still exist. There were brief notes to his family when he was away on his travels, but it was not a writing era, and word of mouth was the normal means of communication. Jesus was not intended to write, but to teach and to set an example that all of us would do well to use as a pattern."

Once again I was prompted to ask why, if Ruth and Jonathan indeed existed and were such devoted followers of Jesus, the New Testament makes no mention of them. I typed the query, and it was Arthur Ford who responded:

"The most dramatic mention of Lazarus concerns his emergence from the tomb, when Jesus commanded him to come forth. Mary and Martha were there, along with the disciples and others who subsequently spread the story of this marvelous happening, but you and Jonathan were not. You were also absent when Mary anointed the feet of Jesus with costly ointment shortly before his crucifixion, and since these are the two main occasions on which my son Lazarus was mentioned in the Good Book, there was no need to mention you.

"But the disciples knew you well, as they knew many other dedicated followers who are not included in the Gospels. I, of course, had passed on before Jesus began his teachings, and thus am also omitted from any mention in the Bible."

Then Lily, who delights in lecturing me, took over the writing: "Since you and Arthur were there in those days, it is fitting that in this life you would feel strong kinship to the New Testament and those whose lives crossed yours. (Arthur Ford was an ordained Disciples of Christ minister in his last earth life, as well as a world-famous medium.) For this reason we would ask you to project the picture of yourself as Ruth, the wife of Jonathan, to the current life and see wherein you are erring now. The sacrifice of goods and services in that life was paramount, and were you to develop a similar habit now of helping those who would spread the word of God in all its ramifications, the good would readily flow.

"Let us then point out some of the qualities that you would be wise to develop in the remainder of this lifetime: gentleness and soft answers, determination to aid those who are less fortunate than self, willingness to put yourself out for others, tenderness toward all who suffer or are heavy-laden, patience, and above all an abiding love for the Godpart in all who cross your path. This, then, will be our sermon for today. But time is fleet, and there remains insufficient time to do all which you would like to accomplish in this present period in physical form. Ponder these words!"

With that grim warning the Guides went on to other subjects, but several weeks later they abruptly wrote: "We will talk a bit more about the Palestinian life, to summarize lessons learned there and point out how they affect your life today. When you devoted yourself to the service of others, you were exhibiting the highest form of achievement, and because of this you have profited in subsequent lives. But when you were forgetting the obligations of home and family in that embodiment, you were simultaneously losing ground. Not until the two melded and the family joined in your pursuits with full hearts did your progress move at an even keel.

"There are many facets to our characters, and while one part progresses at a rapid pace another may pull at the opposite pole, so that there is a ragged appearance when viewed from this side. The aim is to keep the ego or self well balanced, with all segments moving harmoniously together. Develop through meditation the ability to see oneself in the whole, observing which sections are leaving an erose or ragged side that needs tucking in. We should discover which segments need expansion and development, so that we see ourselves somewhat as a globe, with all parts of ourselves rolling forward in perfect attunement. This is not so difficult to do if, when we meditate daily, we glimpse ourselves as a globe and search for the rough edges and the trailing fragments."

Once more before completion of the book, the Guides reverted to that long-ago era, writing: "Let us return to the Palestinian days and speak of the influence Jesus had on those who surrounded him and heard his teachings. Many were those who came to persecute and remained to adore, finding within themselves the power of God the Creator. Jesus was the Christ Spirit incarnate, having derived his powers directly from the Father, being of such purity that none was able to touch him with temptation or blandishment.

"When he drew nigh unto the temple, he was as a light unto darkness, but similar power existed within each soul who sought repentance. Jesus was the catalyst between God and man, and by his shining presence he was able to inspire the sinners, the lame, and the halt to seek the Godself within and perform the cleansing or cure. Thus he employed the laws of God, the inner laws which are at all times able to function through any person who seeks *within* for the Father. 'The kingdom of God is within.' So true! Within each of us is that fount of wisdom that is as readily available to us as the knowledge of right and wrong."

I was reluctant to leave the Palestinian saga without a final word from my "father," Arthur Ford, and in response to my special request he took over the typewriter with a cheery greeting: "Ruth, good work and happy landings! As Jeremiah I learned lessons that have stood me in good stead ever since, though I have not always heeded those essons. Having been so closely drawn to the family that Lazarus headed after my passing, I remained in close touch fter leaving physical form. The radiance of Jesus shone s brightly here as there, and to this day does so. But ad I remained longer in flesh, I hope that I would have rofited through that proximity to the physical ministry f Jesus.

"There are times when all of us seem blind to pportunity, yet always it is there for those who seek purity nd righteousness. When temptations come, as they do ɔ all who inhabit physical bodies, stop to contemplate how ndulgence will blight the record of the soul's progress. ake the long view. Is a passing pleasure worth a karmic ntanglement that will hamper one's future progress until has eventually been erased through atonement?

"This is a practical lesson. View it as selfishly as you ke. The business of living is to achieve perfection, so hy risk internal torment for a passing temptation? Those urdles (temptations) seem mighty low when viewed from iis side, so take them in stride and onward go! Remember hat Lily told you a long time ago. View each day as a erfect whole, vowing to keep it as perfect as a flawless earl. When strung together, such a strand is beautiful ɔ behold, and surely anyone is able to keep one day at time flawless. Make that then the goal."

I did indeed remember Lily's allusion to days as pearls, nd in leafing through the pages of *A Search for the Truth* ɔ review that lesson, I came upon these words that he ad written more than a decade ago:

"Regard each day as an unblemished page in the book f life. The best thing to remember is this: Greet each ay as the untarnished future, and handle it as carefully s if it were already a published record of your past."

If only I could live by that honorable code, I'm sure iat at last I could please the Guides. Nothing less will itisfy them.

BOOK TWO

And Other Lives

13

Group Karma

*It is not more surprising to be born twice than once; everything
in nature is resurrection.*

— VOLTAIRE

To paraphrase Voltaire, it is not
more surprising to be born hundreds of times than twice,
and that is what Edgar Cayce and other famous psychics
declare to be true. Those who accept the doctrine of reincarnation believe we return again and again to physical
body, not only to make amends for previous wrongdoing
but also to live in such a way that we speed our progress
toward eventual reunion with God.

The mystics assert that groups of souls who have known
each other in previous lifetimes tend to return to physical
body at approximately the same time, into circumstances
that permit them again to find each other, in order to
work out karmic relationships. This is called Group Karma,
and Cayce cautioned his followers that unless they were
willing to be linked in lifetime after lifetime with persons
they dislike, they should begin immediately to dissolve the
animosity that forges the bond.

Hate as well as love can therefore bring souls together
again, and Lily and the Guides have written: "On this side
[after death] souls are drawn together by attraction and
like-mindedness, so that there need be no disharmony such

as you encounter in the physical body. Yet the souls wh have met again and again in various incarnations provid such attraction for each other that enemies and rivals ar tied together, as are friends and blood relatives in th flesh. Thus, if you would break those ties of enemy interac tion, it is best to dissolve the bonds in the flesh so tha you do not encounter them time and again. By returnin good for evil, turning the other cheek, and learning t recognize the good qualities of others so that your ange and hatred will die out, these bonds are dissolved or turne into friendships, and the animosity no longer persist Think, then, on this as you encounter those with whom you are not now in harmony."

During Arthur Ford's lifetime he repeatedly told me "I have always believed in reincarnation," and I recentl heard a tape recording of a life reading that a psychi gave for him before his death in which Ford asked, "Wa Ruth Montgomery with me in that particular incarnation? The entranced psychic replied that I was. After Ford physical death, while dictating the material for *A Worl Beyond*, he wrote to me through my typewriter: "We wer friends and comrades, relatives in some lives and not ii others, but never were we rivals or enemies, which is wh we worked so well together and felt such consummate loy alty to each other in the phase I have just finished."

At a later time the Guides wrote: "From the day in age past that you met the soul who later became Arthur Forc you established such a rapport that the tie remaine through all subsequent times. Thus karmic ties can be goo as well as bad, and this is demonstrated by the inspiratio he has always been to you and by the loyalty and affectio you have ever retained toward him; such a kinship tha he has profited by your espousal, as you have advance by association with him. It is always important to under stand these karmic relationships, for they explain other wise-inexplicable situations throughout one's life travel in physical form."

In view of this assertion it seems significant that I, who was a syndicated Washington columnist on politics and world affairs, did not believe in psychic phenomena and communication with the dead until after I met Arthur Ford in 1960.

The Guides stress the importance of trying to recapture memories of past lives so that we can overcome our accumulated faults "and accept conditions which seem not to our liking now, such as infirmities, poverty, weakness, or bad habits." They say we can earn the right to select our parents and the circumstances into which we are born, and that we have usually known family members, friends, and rivals under various circumstances in previous lifetimes. If true, this can explain why we feel such instant rapport with some people on first meeting and such inexplicable dislike for others. The Guides claim that severe suffering or violent deaths in previous lives can cause physical weaknesses and fears in the present embodiment, until we learn to recognize them for what they are and realize that they are simply soul memories. Then we can overcome that hurdle and dismiss it.

There are numerous ways in which we can seek to recapture memories of our past lives. One method is to select an isolated incident from childhood that has for some inexplicable reason made a particularly deep and lasting impression. Then, while in a drowsy state after eating or before falling asleep at night, we can meditate on this incident, using it as a focus to receive impressions from another time and place.

Dreams, particularly those in color, provide another means of producing flashbacks. Tell yourself firmly, just before falling asleep, that you will dream of a past life and will remember it on awakening. If the characters in a dream are wearing costumes of another era and the arena of action is different from any you have known, it is possible that you are reliving scenes from a previous incarnation.

Perhaps the easiest method of recalling "far memories"

is through hypnotic prenatal regression, with a qualified hypnotist taking you backward through time to a period before this life began. In that altered state of consciousness you can seemingly reenact scenes from a previous embodiment, identifying yourself by name and supplying locations and dates. Should you perchance relive a death by falling from a cliff or being buried alive, it could explain your present height phobia, claustrophobia, or other dread, and hopefully rid you of these unnecessary fears. You may also recognize persons then whom you know now, thus gaining new insight into current relationships. And if you physically harmed someone then, it can explain why you may now be suffering from a similar injury.

Readers of my previous psychic books are aware that Lily has been extremely secretive about his own past lives, refusing to divulge any of his various identities. Now, in the material to follow, he opens the door by writing of himself in one lifetime when he claims to have known Arthur Ford, another when he knew me, and a third life that he reportedly shared with both of us. I have no possible means of corroborating these assertions, any more than I can "prove" the lives he attributes to me, although some of them seem to strike a responsive chord. For instance, the Guides discuss three different lifetimes I am said to have spent in ancient Egypt, and I have long felt a close affinity for that fabled land, returning there again and again instead of seeking new places. In fact, it was during my original visit to Egypt in 1952 that I for the first time experienced a vivid sense of *déjà vu* (long before I believed in reincarnation) at the entrance to the Cheops pyramid of Giza.

Fifteen years elapsed before I became convinced of reincarnation and of the equally unproven theory of Group Karma. But Louis Nizer in his best-selling *The Implosion Conspiracy* has this to say: "There is a 'cluster' phenomenon in nature which defies explanation. At infrequent periods in history several geniuses appear at the same time. Usually they know each other. Their fame will last through the centuries. Then a century or two later, another cluster of transcendent, talented men will dominate the scene, and like comets disappear, their like not to blaze across the horizon for hundreds of years. Shakespeare and Bacon are an unforgettable cluster. Leonardo da Vinci and Verrocchio worked together. During their lifetime, Michelangelo and Raphael vied with each other in exhibitions. Da Vinci and Michelangelo compared their work in Florence in 1504. Two centuries later Mozart, Beethoven, Haydn and Schubert. A century later Brahms, Liszt and Schumann. In the philosophical field Voltaire, Rousseau and Diderot. Holmes, Brandeis and Hughes sat on the Supreme Court at the same time."

Many have pondered the extraordinary "coincidence" of such towering statesmen as Thomas Jefferson, George Washington, John Adams, Alexander Hamilton, Benjamin Franklin, and others being available simultaneously at the birth of the Republic. Was it luck, or had they decided to come back together again in order to establish a free nation as an example to all mankind?

And what of the "flowering of New England" in the early nineteenth century, which produced such a glittering array of poets and philosophers as Ralph Waldo Emerson, William Cullen Bryant, Henry David Thoreau, John Greenleaf Whittier, James Russell Lowell, Henry Wadsworth Longfellow, Oliver Wendell Holmes, and Walt Whitman? An accident? The Guides say there is no such thing as an accident, and that groups of souls will return again and again to develop their talents to the highest possible peak, whether that talent be for writing, painting, music, mathematics, statesmanship, or whatever.

"When that talent is fully developed," the Guides declare,

"a soul will perhaps return to applaud the talents of others, learning basic gifts such as simple joy, giving pleasure to one's own family and friends, and finding contentment in unsung labors. Riches come from within, and those who amass too much wealth in one lifetime will return to seek the richness of an inner life or an unadorned existence when the soul grows through sacrifice and love for others. These qualities are as a beacon to others, and through them we learn the art of loving and giving."

Thus the celebrities of earlier eras may be living lives of quiet contemplation today, unknown outside their neighborhoods, while today's VIPs may be the humble ones of another tomorrow. Who knows whether the Romantic poets of England who simultaneously illumined our literature—Blake, Wordsworth, Coleridge, Scott, Byron, Shelley, Keats, and Landor—may not now have formed another "cluster" and be creating an even sweeter melody through gracious, generous living?

Unfortunately there are also recurring "clusters" of evildoers. Trevor Ravenscroft in his remarkable book *The Spear of Destiny* discloses that the leaders of the secret Thule group in Munich, of which Adolf Hitler was one, were Satanists who practiced black magic; and he indicates that these same souls had similarly practiced black arts a thousand years previously. According to Ravenscroft's research, Hitler believed himself to be the reincarnation of Landulf II of Capua (the Klingsor of the anti-Holy Grail group depicted in Richard Wagner's *Parsifal*), whose evil magic involved tortures and human sacrifices. In that life Landulf II had been castrated for raping a noblewoman, and it is interesting to note that Hitler himself was a sadist and sex deviate who was born with only one testicle.

Others in the Thule group recognized themselves and each other as ninth-century anti-Grail people. Hermann Göring claimed to be the reincarnation of Count Boese, a personal friend and confidant of Landulf II; and Dietrich Eckart, Hitler's instructor in black magic who has been termed the "spiritual" founder of Nazism, believed himself to be Bernard of Barcelona, a ninth-century possessor of evil powers.

The Thule group was not the only "cluster" in this period of Nazi supremacy just before World War II. General Helmuth von Moltke, chief of the Imperial General Staff of the German Army, abruptly fell into trance at his desk one day and later revealed that while unconscious he relived a life as Pope Nicholas I in the ninth century. He said he recognized cardinals and bishops of that period as members of the German General Staff, and General von Schlieffen as the scheming Pope Benedict II of a thousand years earlier.

According to Ravenscroft, some of those ninth-century characters returned again in the thirteenth century: Hitler believed himself to have been Count Acerra, lord of Naples and Capri and an evil adept of magic. Göring, who boasted that he always reincarnated with his Führer, claimed to have been Conrad of Marburg, a close associate of Acerra. Joseph Paul Goebbels identified himself as Eckbert of Meran, a thirteenth-century bishop of Bamberg and friend of Acerra. If true, the evil genius of these black-magic adepts has repeatedly, during the course of history, disrupted affairs of state and attempted to block the upward progress of mankind.

Thus the old saw, "You can't take it with you," applies only to fame and fortune. What we *do* take with us is our karma, whether bad or good, to plague or bless us in future incarnations.

CHAPTER

14

Moab (Circa 1500 B.C.*)*

The Guides, *having amiably agreed to study the akashic records in order to tell me about previous lives that Arthur Ford and I allegedly shared, pursued the subject with dogged determination. Unfortunately, however, they exhibited little interest in pursuing one life at a time. Since* time *means nothing on the other side, they skipped about from one period to another, sometimes hopelessly confusing me about which life was under discussion until I would insist that they identify the subject matter. This they would agreeably do, but they gaily left me to sort out the segments and fit together the jigsaw puzzle of human relationships.*

Because of my unquenchable interest in the mythical lost continent of Atlantis, in whose "reality" I believed from the moment of first hearing about it, I hoped the Guides would provide some fascinating documentation about life in that fabled domain. But as the months passed and only a few tantalizing references were made to Atlantis, I finally asked the Guides if I had lived there, and if so, please to tell me about it.

Their reply was blunt and to the point. "Of course you lived in Atlantis, and so did Arthur Ford," they wrote, "but the two of you were not there at the same time, so it does not belong in this account." Swallowing my disappointment, I then permitted them to proceed in their own distinctive way.

Now that they have completed their dictation about the parallel lives Arthur and I reportedly shared, it would seem that the first recorded one—and the dullest—occurred in the land of Moab, since the encyclopedia "guesses" that the Exodus of Jews from Egypt happened in the fifteenth or sixteenth century before Christ.

The Guides launched the story of that life in rather curious fashion, declaring:

For a long time you have been ailing from a variety of nervous tensions. These are manifested in many ways, including the back and leg muscles, and the fingers, which break out at the nerve endings. The reasons for this are diverse, but principally the trouble stems from a previous life when you were in a barren wasteland, without prospects of adventure or mental development. This was in the land of Moab when the Exodus had been completed. There you toiled as a laborer in the fields, for you were a man, and the going was not easy. Within you dwelt a high-spirited soul, but lacking expression for it, you felt stymied and dull.

This was a testing period, since you had previously had many advantages in some lives. But in this particular one you were on your mettle, so to speak, to prove that this tedious existence could be borne with patience and good spirit. The soul was sorely tempted to depart that life, although you managed to remain imprisoned in an unwelcome body until death came naturally. However, those inner tensions are still reflected when you feel nonproductive and wonder if you are doing all that you are able to fulfill your destiny.

In that life you fathered several children, but conditions were such that you scarcely seemed to know them, for they too worked in the fields and fell asleep as soon as they had supped. Your name then was Nathan, and your wife, who died in childbirth from exhaustion and neglect, was called Madia. Now that you know this, free the tensions and let them drift lazily apart from your being, for there is no need for them in this current interesting and exciting life.

* * *

Easier said than done, I growled to myself on reading those words. Even as I typed, two of my fingers were splotched with blisters that no doctor has been able to cure for long. The blisters have a habit of appearing when I am under tension or pressure, and readers of my previous books must be tired of hearing about the problem of muscular spasms in my back. Well, at least in one life I was apparently able to perform back-breaking toil.

Referring to that incarnation on a subsequent day, the Guides wrote:

Arthur Ford was another workman in the fields who gave you glimpses into that which was missing from the thought of the times. That hard work in Moab from sunup to sundown was not the substance of life, and Arthur's insights opened windows of your mind and made it possible for you to bear the boredom, which otherwise would have set you back in spiritual and inner development.

Perhaps my subconscious was flashing some inner doubts about what they were writing, because they abruptly declared:

This life that we tell you of is true! Arthur at that time was a neighboring worker who often labored alongside you in the fields, a man as hard-pressed as you were. And the friendship waxed strong, for the hours spent in the fields were the longest and most meaningful in that life. He let you talk of your dreams and inner promptings, and the release was good for your entrapped soul. He too shared those dreams and hopes of a better time to come.

In all, it was not a wasted life, but one of suspension.

I have no doubt that the Guides would have continued to give me details of that life if I had asked, but I could not bear to think about it. Enough was enough.

Chapter

15

Egypt (Circa 1390 B.C.*)*

*T*he Guides during a period of several *months assigned three Egyptian lives to Arthur and me. In each of them I was of the feminine gender, and after reading about that dreary embodiment in Moab, when I was said to be a man, I welcomed the change.*

They began their account of my earliest Egyptian life by declaring that when I was a little girl in Thebes, "The sun shone with a brilliance that has always made you yearn, in subsequent incarnations, for sunshine."

At least the latter portion of this statement is true, because although my skin is too fair for sunbathing, I am such a worshiper of sunshine that we moved to Mexico in pursuit of it after my husband retired. To continue the narrative, the Guides next wrote:

There along the Nile you lived and played and wandered among the pillars of Karnak. The beauty of the statuary and the splendor of the arcades filled you with rapture, and because your father was a priest in the temple, your presence was accepted in the area of the colonnades. Ptolmey was the name of your father, the soul whom you later knew as Arthur Ford; and your mother was Carmi, a priestly woman with courtly ways and intelligent mien. She was fond of you and her other little ones, but more interested in devotions and the ritual of the temple, so that you were left free to develop in your own way. This gave you opportunity to develop without too much hindrance from adults, and so you willingly chose to become a student, that you might feel the governing hand of the scholars. Ever it is thus, that when education is forced on children they are apt to resent it, but when discipline is lacking they crave it, as flowers the dew.

When your father (Arthur Ford) would take you on his knee to give you the rudiments of philosophy, you liked best to hear tales of the Atlanteans who forsook their island kingdom to spread the word of its wonders, before the flood engulfed that noble land. And wondrous were the stories that he told you, for he had met some of the priests who were descended from Atlanteans on his journeys to Heliopolis and the pyramids nearby.

This was one of those tantalizing references to Atlantis that had led me to believe the Guides would tell me about my "own" life there. But such was not to be, and the next day they resumed:

When you were older, your father Ptolmey (Ford) took you down the Nile to see the splendors of that ancient area. The gods that you then worshiped were many, and you felt a certain superstition about them, but asked too many questions to suit the priests: Why should the duties of the gods encompass so many simple pastimes? Why were some said to be more powerful than others? Who decides which gods and goddesses shall do which? Then who is the overall god? For someone has to make decisions.

The priests were nonplussed by your questions and felt that you should be punished for such blasphemy, but your father (Arthur Ford) was secretly amused, for he too questioned the idiocy of such widespread worship of so many differing gods. Thus when Amenhotep IV received the scepter of power in Egypt, it was with relief to you and your father that he cast out the old gods, building a new center of worship down the Nile from Thebes (at Tell el-amarna), where he established the authority of the One God.

These were joyful times for you, and when a center of learning was also established there, you and some of your brothers were permitted to study the higher philosophies and mathematics. You believed in the One God with all your being, and so did the man who much later became Arthur Ford. Then trouble arose, for many others were not willing to forsake their gods, who had seemingly brought them good luck and fertility; thus they split up into factions, so that there was feuding and even rebellion in the land.

You were ever antagonistic toward those whom you considered to be beneath your mental prowess, and you showed scorn toward those who could not easily accept the premise of the One God who oversaw all the land and His creations. In this strife that arose you were a ring leader of the Amenhotep faction, and when the pharaoh fell from power, you fell too. Humility you lacked, and thus you returned again and again to physical body to learn that lesson.

Rereading this account several times, I recalled the deep impression Karnak and Thebes had made on me some years ago when my husband and I were there. I had yearned to proceed down the Nile to the site of the city Amenhotep had carved out of the desert, even though friends told me there was little to see, but because Bob had no interest in it, we flew back to Cairo. I therefore asked the Guides for more information about this period in Egyptian history and they moved ahead to "my" adult years, writing:

Your husband in that life was in the service of Pharaoh Ikhnaton, as Amenhotep now became known, and you were one of the ladies-in-waiting to his wife, Nefertiti. As we said earlier, you had shifted your allegiance to Aton, the One God, while many others ranted and raged and continued to worship Amon secretly. The times were hard, and the issues split families and friends.

During that period when you were serving with Pharaoh's family in the new city, you came to know them well. Nefertiti was exquisite beyond belief, in your opinion, and you were fond of her although sometimes afraid of her sharp tongue and regal ways. Tutankhamen (or Tutenkhamon) you knew in his childhood and early youth, and you thought him effeminate and childish, but sweet and mannerly.

Ikhnaton was fanatical in his devotion to the One God. Had he been more willing to live and let live, he would not have divided his kingdom so sharply, but he was fiercely determined to establish the rule of Aton and abolish the old gods too suddenly for success. Yet his name lives forever as the first ruler to recognize and worship one God, and who will deny that such an act that lives forever in the minds of those to follow is more effective than to have popularity in one's own lifetime? After Ikhnaton met his death, you and your husband eventually returned to Thebes, where your property had been confiscated, but because of Tutankhamen's remembrance of your kindnesses, you were permitted to live again in the royal compound, where he was now the Pharaoh.

No mention had been made of Arthur Ford for some time, but one day the Guides began the session, as if weeks had not elapsed since the last reference to this life, by writing:

To return to your father, Ptolmey, who later became Arthur Ford; he despised human sacrifices as you did, and the new religion of Aton opened a brilliant window on the dawning of a new age of mercy and freedom. He influenced Ikhnaton to free slaves and to teach love and compassion so that all might stand as equals. But the nobility opposed this revolutionary new theory and fought for restoration of their original rights as privileged citizens. They secretly worshiped the old gods and sought to turn the Pharaoh from his ways. And because enemies of Egypt seized this opportune time to encroach on its territory and trade routes, the stake was great.

Ikhnaton wished to prevent bloodshed in war as well as in peace, so the defenses were negligible, and the soldiers, backed by the nobility, sought to overthrow Ikhnaton before the country itself perished as a separate entity. Ikhnaton felt himself deserted even by his One God toward the end of that reign, and was so despised by the people that on his death his new city, carved out of the wilderness along the Nile, was allowed to perish as well. The court returned to Thebes, and you among them, although there was no particular welcome for you there because of your worship of Aten with heart and soul . . . as well as mouth.

Arthur (Ptolmey) was put to death by the jealous priests of Aton and you grieved at his passing, but there was such turmoil in those times that many were being put to death. There was little regret among the people when you suffered death from a plague that seemed to have been carried back by soldiers returning from war in Syria. Many were those who perished from that plague.

In that life you advanced spiritually through your grasp of the concept of the One God, but those who survived did not lament your passing, for you were outspoken about your beliefs and too intolerant of those who were unable to grasp that concept.

Feeling rather sorry for myself, since the Guides always seem so critical of me, I asked for further comment on that intriguing period of history, and they wrote:

In that Egyptian life during the reign of Amenhotep we find a man known in these present times as Judge John Sirica (shades of Watergate!), a judge also in those days and one who was dedicated to the One God. He ruled against factions who sought to overthrow Amenhotep, or Ikhnaton, as he was then called, and return to the worship of many gods, but he too was scorned by the people and eventually lost his life, as did Ptolmey (Arthur Ford), in the bloody uprising against the Pharaoh.

Do you not remember the man you now know as Senator Barry Goldwater in Thebes? He was of the priestly cult who assisted Arthur Ford in the temple, and after Arthur moved his family to the new seat of government with

Amenhotep, he followed shortly, serving there with good nature and devotion. He was not a warrior, but when Egypt was invaded during this period, he took up arms in defense of the nation and fell on the field of battle beside the man who was much later to be known as George Patton. A good man and true!

The Egyptian life ended for you through plague. You had wandered for a time before settling at the palace in Thebes to serve Tutankhamen's new queen. There you became ill and were moved to the House of Life, a sort of hospital, where you died. What did you learn from that life? That there is One God, but that many are unwilling to dedicate themselves to God when disfavor threatens, and you yourself had to turn your back on the precept of the One because it was now illegal to worship Him. Amon was restored to power along with the multitudinous other gods, and the joy went out of your life when this became the law. Secretly you continued to believe in the One God who rules all things, but never were you permitted to say so in public.

Arthur Ford as a priest of the One God refused to return to the cult of Amon and was consequently beheaded in the city of Aton (Akhetaton), without returning to Thebes. You admired his courage and secretly bowed before the Living God, who had no statue or other sign of His existence.

After reviewing this material, I came to the reluctant conclusion that the character I am said to have been came off second best to Arthur Ford. He had died for his faith, whereas I met an ignominious death by plague after trying to save my neck by silence concerning my beliefs. Never once, in all the material the Guides have provided, did they assign a hero's death to me. I rather envied Arthur!

CHAPTER

16

Egypt (Circa 1300 B.C.*)*

The first Egyptian life that the Guides recorded may have influenced my alleged embodiment as Ruth in Palestine, where I again abandoned the established faith to become Christian. But as we shall later see, this second life along the Nile is said to have wielded tremendous influence not only on a nineteenth-century lifetime in England but also on my present one. At least in this particular incarnation I seemed to have moved up a step in the social ladder, because the Guides wrote:

As a princess in Egypt around 1300 B.C. the tradition existed that a woman pharaoh was bad luck for the country, and because you were first in line for the throne, there were those who would destroy you. You were seventeen and ripe for marriage when those who thought they were protecting the best interests of the country managed to surprise you one day, as you were standing on an outlook above the Nile basin; and in an unguarded moment when your ladies-in-waiting were gathering herbs, they bribed one to shove you to your death.

In the unexpected fall your back was broken, and for days you lived in agony until death mercifully relieved you of all suffering and responsibility. Thus, if you would free yourself from constant back problems now, remember that incident which created no karmic problem for you personally, since all that befell you was of another's doing. See it as a minor plague in a long line of happy lives, depending on how you view adversities. Cast it from you in this instant! Your back is free from karmic or invidious ties to the past and has no physical cause in this one. Lift your mind above it, and walk with free and vibrant stride. Go in good health, and forgive all who have ever harmed you.

There was that back again! And perhaps this second Egyptian lifetime explains my current height phobia, which I first became aware of at the age of seven after I climbed with a friend to the dome of the county courthouse in Princeton, Indiana. I cannot bear to ride up mountains on ski lifts, look straight down from high buildings, or ride in helicopters, although airplanes fortunately do not bother me, since the outlook from the windows is out instead of directly down.

Since it isn't every day that I get to be a princess, I urged the Guides to supply further details about that exotic-sounding life in the days before women's liberation could have fought for my right to succession, and this is what they wrote:

In that Egyptian life as a princess you met an untimely death because you were a woman, and the ruling clique preferred a man to succeed your father as pharaoh. Your brother Ramses, whom you now call Arthur Ford, was three years younger than you, and a delight to the court as well as to you. A sturdy boy with large vision, he wanted to be pharaoh, although he loved you very much and was in a quandry as to how he might succeed without hurting the rightful heiress to the ancient throne. You also longed to be pharaoh, and although pride was strong in you both, yet did you adore each other, and already you were planning how best to use the talents of your brother in the next highest post. You were of marriageable age, and since at that time society looked with horror on the idea of brother and sister marrying (although at some periods in Egyptian history this was the custom), there was no thought of you and Ramses becoming man and wife to rule side by side on the throne of Egypt.

One day Ramses said to you, in a tone he hoped sounded jocular, "Sister, why should you be burdened with the heavy scepter of office when I am strong enough to carry it for both of us?"

Smiling, you replied that since you were the elder, it might be well for you to carry the scepter at least until he was at an age to handle it alone, for he was barely into his teens. Neither of you seriously considered the conversation; yet it set other minds to working and plotting, and when an elder statesman suggested that you rule only until your brother was twenty, it infuriated you, for he was asking you to surrender your birthright. Thus, with your father, the old Pharaoh, lying on his deathbed, the plotters decided to take affairs into their own hands.

Good heavens, I wondered, did my old pal Arthur Ford do me in? But apparently not, because after repeating in somewhat different words the horrendous events that led to my early demise, the Guides wrote:

Ramses was not aware of the plot and did not realize that you had been tricked, for it appeared as an accident, and although a young boy, he stepped easily into the shoes of your father. Arthur Ford, your brother Ramses in that life, lived to a happy old age, thinking often of the sister whom he had loved, and totally unaware she was a victim of foul play. After all, the other women were not within range of vision when the deed occurred, and the attendant who performed the act was soon put away by those who had bribed her to do it.

I felt mollified, but still somewhat cheated. Just as I had missed being mentioned in the New Testament, now I had lost my recorded place in Egyptian history as a Pharaoh! Somewhat later I sought to find reference to Arthur Ford's Egyptian incarnation in the encyclopedia. To my consternation, I learned that there had been twelve pharaohs named Ramses (or Rameses), but after reading the various accounts, it seemed that Arthur most nearly fitted into the slot of Ramses II, "who succeeded his father Seti at an early age and reigned sixty-seven years" until his death. If so, Arthur was one of the greatest builders of the ancient world, which seems rather incongruous. Yet the Guides insisted that he succeeded to the throne as a boy and "lived to a happy old age."

Loath to have missed such an exciting reign, I asked what purpose my own alleged life had served, and the Guides replied:

Every incarnation serves an important purpose, no matter if it lasts but a few days and repays some trailing karma. In that life along the Nile you learned many things that have since stood you in good stead: love, gaiety, optimism, and consideration for those beneath you in material advantage. Yet the soul memory of that aching broken back has continued to plague you in other lives. Thus it is important now for you to understand that this is a subconscious memory and has no part in your present lifetime. It should be aired, as we have done here, and then forgotten.

17

Persia (Circa 800 B.C.)

*T*he Guides, as reported earlier, had
*a madcap habit of jumping daily from one period of history to
another, giving bits and pieces of a life in Greece, England,
or Egypt and returning to them again and again. Since I have
sorted them into some semblance of chronological order, I will
therefore leave the third Egyptian story that they recorded until
later and go now to an incarnation that seemingly occurred some
eight hundred years before Jesus changed the course of history.*

*My spirit pen pals gave no date for this incarnation, but because
it is an era that allegedly precedes Zoroaster by a generation,
and no one knows the time of his birth, I have arbitrarily assigned
an approximate date for the sake of convenience. It may be a
couple of hundred years off in either direction, as no two authorities
agree on the exact time when Zoroastrianism, the religion of
Persia, was founded.*

*This particular "lifetime" was interesting to me because the
Guides brought into it a number of people I know today. This
is the way they began:*

At the city in the hills and plains of ancient Persia you
knew Edgar Cayce and Elsie Sechrist. The woman who
became Elsie Sechrist in her present embodiment was then
as a ministering angel to all about her and invaluable in
her assistance to the man Uhjltd, who would eventually
become Cayce.

You were also one of the assistants to Uhjltd, the doctor-
priest, and in that city near present-day Shushtar, Iran, you

handled patients, and often did you purge and bleed them, as you were somewhat of a nurse. But the herbs interested you more than the physical treatments, for the skillful blending of these medications fascinated those of you who had first understood them in ancient Egypt, and some even in Atlantis.

At least I could understand my preference for herbs to physical treatment. In my present embodiment, I confess that I can scarcely bear to be around those who are sick. What a contrast to Elsie Sechrist, author of Dreams—Your Magic Mirror, *who before her marriage was a head nurse at Bellevue Hospital in New York City. Elsie, in a life reading given for her by Edgar Cayce shortly before his death in 1945, was told that she had assisted him in his Persian life as Uhjltd and also in an earlier incarnation when he was Ra-ta in Egypt. He said her name then was Lido-la. Addressing me, the Guides wrote:*

In Persia you were called Helmadere and you were a woman. Ever have you been happier as a woman than a man. You were helpful and full of sympathy for the suffering; yet this was not the total range of your interest, for you were also fascinated by the heavens and by archaeology. You studied the stars under magi and astrologers, and besought those of wiser mien to teach you the hidden lore of earth and sky.

It is interesting to note that large-scale excavations are now under way by archaeologists around Shushtar, Iran, which both Cayce and the Guides identified as the one-time city in the hills and the plains.

There were those in high authority in those times who would have thwarted the work of Uhjltd (Cayce) and those of you who devoted your lives to his teachings. The problems were therefore acute, but all of you surmounted them and continued the work, sometimes in caves concealed from passersby, although those of the vicinity were acquainted with the topography and knew where to find you.

The soul Adelle Davis, as she is known in this lifetime, was in that Persian embodiment an adept who assisted Cayce and others in their evaluation of herbs and the preparation thereof. She played an active role in the maintenance of proper diet for those who had to live in caves during the onslaughts of invading hordes, and she was able to foretell from omens. Her interest now in diets and foods stems partly from that life and also from another in Egypt when she knew Edgar Cayce as Ra-ta and was active in overseeing the intake of food and medication by patients in the temple. She was called Evanessa in Persia and Ruena in Egypt.

The mention of my good friend Adelle Davis in this connection was intriguing. Not only is she America's best-known nutritionist and the author of several best-selling books including Let's Get Well, *she also has a healthy interest in psychic matters. Some years ago I introduced her when she lectured at Edgar Cayce headquarters in Virginia Beach for the Association for Research and Enlightenment.*

This was a strenuous life when you lived in a cave, as did many others, for there were dissensions among the tribes, and invaders were so numerous that as you helped those who ailed, you also required protection from the invaders. The entity now known as Evalyn Dolph was then about your age, and she revered the man Ketolfr, who in his present life is King Hussein of Jordan. He was of godly mien, and so adored by the people that he was a leader among men, as he is today.

* * *

*Evalyn (Mrs. William B.) Dolph is a Cuernavaca friend of
mine who used to live in Washington, D.C. Becoming interested
in reincarnation after reading my books on the subject, she recently
submitted to hypnosis in order to tap into a past incarnation.
While hypnotically regressed, she seemed to relive a life in a cave
somewhere in the Middle East; she was not sure where. Afterward
she commented that she had never felt as happy as she did while
experiencing that lifetime and that she had "recognized" King
Hussein as a revered friend, although he did not resemble his
current photographs. I know the brave young king of Jordan,
having met him at the White House and also at his palace in
Amman, but Evalyn has not met him, and she was aware of
no interest in him until she "saw" him while in that altered state
of consciousness.*

Ketolfr (Hussein) and Uhjltd (Cayce) were of one mind
in their determination to lead the people out of poverty
and sickness and to promulgate the ideal of the unity of
mankind. Although few at that time were able to grasp
the significance of the Law of One, they nevertheless
needed spiritual guidance, and this was given in full
measure by Cayce, Hussein, and others. Elsie Sechrist was
outstanding in her role as an assistant to Cayce in treating
physical as well as spiritual needs, and Ketolfr (Hussein)
at that time was of a priestly order who counseled those
needing guidance. Evalyn Dolph was devoted to him and
willing to follow wherever he directed, and they worked
in perfect harmony. This was a happy life for her, with
spiritual growth and development as she learned to
meditate and to serve.

*Next the Guides introduced into that Persian life the extraordi-
nary "magnetic healer" whom I called Mr. A in my book about
him titled* Born to Heal. *In his present life Mr. A can seemingly*

heal almost any ailment, ranging from cancer to glaucoma, by
sending what he calls "life energies" to the magnetic field (the
lower abdomen) of his patients through his own fingertips. He
calls this method "the ancient wisdom." The Guides wrote of him:

In that Persian era the man you now call Mr. A was
an outstanding healer who worked alongside Uhjltd
(Cayce) in the city in the hills and the plains, and oftentimes
they communicated by mental telepathy when the advice
or counsel of one was needed by the other. He was highly
developed for his times, and indeed for any age, and he
automatically knew which herbs had poisonous qualities
and which were beneficial. He loved to demonstrate his
prowess in taming wild animals simply by his own vibrations, and to make assistants of wolves, which he taught
to warn him of approaching storms or dangers. Jolly and
beneficial in his influence, he worked well with Cayce in
those far-off times when each was closer to nature and
God than men have been in later millennia.

I have already written of Mr. A that in his present incarnation
he has an amazing way with animals and that he has a "trigger
stomach" which automatically "brings up" any food that has been
"contaminated" by preservatives or insect sprays.

Arthur Ford in the Persian embodiment was your son,
but although he knew Cayce and the man you now call
Mr. A, during his boyhood he roamed afar, joining the
caravans that linked present-day Shushtar with the entire
Tigris and Euphrates crescent. Thus he was not often at
home as he grew toward manhood. When his caravan was
seized by Greek invaders and he was imprisoned, he sought
to communicate through mental telepathy with those of
you at home. But he died of desert fever in a dungeon
before his twenty-first year.

*   *   *

Thus far the Guides had described lives in which Arthur Ford had been known to me as father, brother, and friend. Now he was my "son," and this time I was outliving him. The Guides were apparently content to abandon him in his wretched tomb, because they made no further reference to him. Eventually I asked for more information about the lad who met such a sad death when barely out of his teens, and they obligingly wrote:

Arthur in that life was adventurous and eager to know all that was going on in the world. He was interested in the work of Uhjltd (Cayce) and the others and sought to understand the laws governing psychic communication. Yet he felt stultified in the small-town atmosphere. He was stimulated by the colorful caravans with their exotic wares and by the strange people who traveled throughout the then-known world of the East.

He enjoyed the dash of danger until he was seized by the invaders and plunged into a dungeon. Then it was that he sought to put to use that which he had learned about mental telepathy, but his time had come to abandon the body, for before beginning that life he had pledged to return to understand more of the workings of the inner self. Although he was not eager to abandon the body, yet it was his destiny, for in some of his other lives he had wrought havoc on the plans of others, particularly as Ramses in Egypt, where many died because of his insistence on building huge statues to himself.

In that Persian life he was atoning by being a "nobody" and through his travels he was learning that all peoples have similar aspirations and love of beauty, if given half a chance; that each person dearly loves life and does not willingly lay it down at the behest of a ruler who is seeking self-aggrandizement.

This was the first time the Guides had critized Arthur, or practically anyone except me, and I found it rather refreshing.

But since the dictation was a joint effort by "Lily, Art, and the Group," apparently Arthur had done some soul-searching during the periods between earth lives when he was in spirit form. To return to the narrative:

That Persian life was one of dedication to an ideal—developing new methods for healing the sick—and when caravans passed through what would now be Shuster, the supplies not available in that area of Persia were purchased from them. The caravan merchants exchanged their precious ointments for the herbs and blendings of medicines that the soul Cayce had divined. You were a close-knit group who worked together there, and many were the times that the work seemed destined to be abandoned because of persecutions. The great work continued, although it ended for many of you when you were killed in an invasion which destroyed some of that which had been fashioned from faith.

Slaughter and rapine devastated the area, but though the physical bodies lay covered with blood, there was rejoicing in the plane where we (the Guides) are now, since the good had outlived the bad, and the worthwhileness of that life was apparent to all. When the perils of invasion had vanished from the land, there evolved a high state of medical awareness which the people had learned from the soul Cayce and those of you who had assisted him with herbs and medication, so that this knowledge was not discarded or lost. It was eternally preserved among the descendants of that race with whom you all worked.

Uhjltd (Cayce) and some of the others lived on for many years, but the entity now known as Adelle Davis, who had led an active and useful life, was killed in the Greek invasion that also ended your own life.

During my brief sojourn in Virginia Beach I heard that Edgar Cayce while in trance had told something of a former life when

he was Uhjltd in the city in the hills and the plains, and tha
he gave as its location the present site of Shushtar, Iran. I wa.
vaguely aware that he had claimed some connection with Zoroaster
who inspired the Persian religion known as Zoroastrianism, bu
that was the extent of my knowledge.

After reading this material from the Guides, I therefor
researched some of Cayce's readings, in which he said that Uhjlt
(himself) had two sons called Zend and Ujndt. Cayce reporte
that Zend fathered Zoroaster, and that many centuries later th
soul known as Zend reincarnated as Jesus of Nazareth. Ther
is no conceivable way, at least in our present state of awareness
to verify these astonishing statements. But since the Guides ha
said I knew Jesus in Palestine, I asked whether I had also know
Zend or Zoroaster in the so-called Persian life, and they wrote.

Zend, the son of Uhjltd, was noble in visage, attainment
and perception; somewhat of a dreamer, for he was no
of the practical turn of mind of his brother, Ujndt. Zenc
was a forerunner of Jesus, the same soul in a differen
body. But as Zend, the Christ Spirit had not yet descendec
on him, so that he was then still a striving soul seeking
perfection. He was not yet the Savior, for that would come
in his incarnation as Jesus of Nazareth.

You did not know Zoroaster, the harbinger of a grea
age in Persia, because you met death before his birth. Zenc
you knew, but you were more nearly the age of Zoroaster'
grandfather, Uhjltd, who later became Edgar Cayce. Ir
that life you worked closely with those who assisted ir
the work of Uhjltd, and to the extent that you formulatec
new ideas in connection with herbal treatments and the
knitting of bones, you were of substantial service to others

At first it seemed odd that so many people I know today were
said by the Guides to have shared this alleged incarnation in
ancient Persia. But not according to Edgar Cayce, for while
researching his material about that era, I learned that of the

twenty-five hundred individuals for whom he gave life readings, more than four hundred were told they had been associated with the Persian activities of Uhjltd and Zend, whom he claimed to have been an earlier incarnation of Jesus. If true, this supports the thesis of group karma: that throngs of souls return to physical being at the same time in order to resolve their karmic ties or enjoy each other's company.

While perusing the readings about Uhjltd, I was gratified to learn that Cayce too had told of numerous uprisings and invasions in that Persian era, some by Greek tribes. Pleased that what the Guides had written seemed to check out so well with other sources, I was beginning to pride myself on having been such a high-minded and useful person in that life when the Guides, in their inimitable manner, wrote:

Then, as now, subservience was not among your virtues. You valued the opinions of others only so long as they gave you new insights or coincided with your own views. Seldom did you forget self while serving others. Try, Ruth, try to develop this quality and you will have surmounted a real barrier to your spiritual advancement.

Well, you can't win 'em all!

18

Egypt (Circa 300 B.C.)

*A*rthur Ford in his present spirit state *seems as loath as I have always been to leave Egypt. He and the Guides returned again and again to the subject of that ancient kingdom, to provide additional information about the parallel lives that we supposedly spent there. They began their account of the third Egyptian incarnation like this:*

In the Egyptian life of which we now write you were the daughter of Periclesis, who governed an area of some prominence not far from the Nile delta. As a small child you played with other children along the mighty river, sailing little boats made from papyrus and being taken out in sailing vessels which seemed to you as vast as ocean liners would today. A trip along the Nile to Alexandria was the most exciting thing that had ever happened to you, and you adored the sea near your parents' new house in Alexandria.

There you dreamed of foreign lands across the boundaries of the Mediterranean and thrived on tales of those exotic places where others had been: Jaffa, Athens, Italy, and even Spain and what is now Portugal. There were tales of the great island of Poseidia (Atlantis), which had sunk beyond the gates of Hercules, and to you the world was an exciting, fascinating, fabulous land peopled with pirates and scholars, explorers and shopkeepers.

To all this you added a vivid imagination, so that even

the land below the sea seemed peppered with secrets of lost civilizations and towering moguls who ruled the bottom of the earth. Your father was advanced in thinking for his times, and because you early exhibited delight in acquiring knowledge, he permitted you to study at the famed library in Alexandria, when the family was occupying its house beside the sea for long stretches at a time.

Arthur Ford was a friend of your parents, and because he recognized the value of such an imagination as yours, he put it to work in directed channels, so that no subject seemed closed to you. He gave supervision to your studies and research at the library, and your parents felt no qualms about permitting you freedom to open your mind to the realities of the far vaster world outside Egypt.

Ford had traveled to much of the Middle East, and his stories delighted you, since they were ever of ancient lores and customs, rather than gossip of society and the bazaars. Thus he became your mentor and guiding light, and when once he spoke to you about his theories of reincarnation, you eagerly accepted them as your own beliefs, understanding that he had been a man of towering strength in previous lives, which had cemented your friendship.

This was the second lifetime in which the Guides had spoken of my vivid imagination, and again I began to have qualms about whether this imagination was now creating fantasies about former incarnations. Because I have always been dedicated to truth, the possibility greatly disturbed me. Yet where could I have obtained so much factual material of which I am unaware? Whenever I challenge the Guides and try to prove them wrong, I find that they are correct in their historical data, and some scholars have suggested that the best way to probe history and prehistoric times is through hypnotic regression of souls who assertedly lived then. Others aver that we are able under certain conditions to experience cosmic consciousness, or race memory. If so, that seems as remarkable as communicating with souls who have passed on.

Arthur Ford, whose name then was Demorathage, spoke sometimes of a land beyond Gibraltar which had sunk into the Atlantic in a great upheaval of earth and waters many millennia before, and through research in the library you read testimony that eminent scholars had handed down concerning the worth of that kingdom and its influence on Egypt when visitors from there came to your native country before Poseidia at last sank into the sea. Bas-reliefs and sculptures depicting natives of Atlantis were used as a motif in many of the papyrus ledgers, and even in some tombs, for there were those who claimed to be direct descendants of Atlantean priests and travelers, and they held themselves a cut above those who could not offer similar claims to their origin.

True it was that the Atlanteans had been far more advanced in civilization than had the early Egyptians, whom they sought to instruct in their ways. Ford had studied the subject, and he encouraged you in your pursuit of additional knowledge from archives whenever available to become an authority on that ancient culture.

This information sent me to the encyclopedia, where I learned that after Alexander the Great conquered Egypt in 332 B.C. he combined some old towns into one and named it Alexandria. Shortly thereafter Ptolemy I founded the great library of Alexandria, where manuscripts were collected from all parts of the then-known world. Under his son Ptolemy Philadelphus, the Alexandrine library rapidly became the intellectual center of Hellenistic culture. As the city gradually declined in political importance during the next several hundred years, the library waned and eventually was destroyed.

Arthur Ford was a scholar of world renown for those ancient days, and had you not met him through your parents, your life would have been entirely different, for in you he awakened the yearning for all knowledge. Although you spent the days in deep study, you had a joyous nature which fitted well with that of the scholar Arthur, who was a merry gentleman despite his vast knowledge of books and places. As you grew older, under his tutelage you amassed so great a fund of awareness that although it was unusual for women in those days to have such an education, you became an assistant to Ford. Demorathage, as he was called, had a large and happy family who dwelt also in Alexandria beside the sea.

One day at his house you met a shining and erudite young man whom you know today as Hugh Lynn Cayce, and there was mutual attraction, for you had known him—always pleasantly—in other lives. It was like enveloping a dearly beloved friend to set eyes on him for the first time in that life, and there was mutual soul recognition between you which led to an early marriage. The wedding took place at the house of your parents in Alexandria. Then you and he set out by boat for Heliopolis in the environs of present-day Cairo, where he worked in an advisory capacity to the Macedonian rulers. He was not the top adviser, but was a knowledgeable man with keen perception and good education. Staophus, as he was known then, was older than you by seven years, and the marriage was a good one, although you missed the silence of the library and the worlds it opened to your eager mind.

Hugh Lynn Cayce is, of course, the son of America's most famous seer and president of the Association for Research and Enlightenment, an organization founded to carry on the teachings of Edgar Cayce. The Guides next introduced the name of a woman whom I now know as the director of our excellent English-language library at the Episcopal Guild in Cuernavaca, Mexico, writing:

Anne Wenck was a friend of yours in the library at Alexandria in Egypt and took much responsibility, for she was highly evolved. Her name was Aesopholus, and she was an overseer of the library who assisted with guidance for those who researched and studied there. She was helpful in your research on Atlantis and took a personal interest in your pursuit, for she too was intensely interested in the old legends about Atlantis and was a scholarly authority on Plato.

Older than you, she was a particular friend of Arthur Ford's wife. She was a kindly, intelligent woman with great powers of concentration until she injured her leg so badly when struck by a cart in the crowded streets that she suffered greatly. But this should not trouble the present entity, Anne Wenck, when she realizes that it is a soul memory rather than a present physical problem. She also knew Hugh Lynn Cayce when you met and married him, and although she was unmarried, she took great interest in young people, particularly as related to development of their eager young minds.

Since I knew Mrs. Wenck only slightly at the time of this message, and she walks normally, I asked her if she was aware of any leg problem. "Am I!" she exclaimed. "Even as a small child my sister said she could always tell my approach by the sound of my walk, because I seemed to drag one leg. I've never limped, but I have had a circulatory problem with it for many years."

When I told her what had come through my typewriter from the Guides about the cause of the trouble, she declared, "When I was a child of about five in Northumberland, Pennsylvania, I was almost run down by a horse-drawn cart on the main street. My parents thought I would be killed, but I managed to slip past it in the nick of time." With an apologetic chuckle, she added, "I can't tell you how many times in the years since then I've remembered the unreasoning pride I felt in escaping that cart. It has long embarrassed me, to think that as a child I thought

*I was so smart!" This could well be due to a soul memory stemming
from the tragedy of a similar happening in a previous life, since
the normal reaction for most of us who have had narrow escapes
is simply one of relief.*

*Knowing nothing of Mrs. Wenck's background, I had assumed
that she was an accomplished librarian before moving to this retire-
ment community, because in the three years since becoming the
unpaid director of a fledgling library operated solely by volunteers,
she has quadrupled it in size and so greatly improved its quality
that it is an invaluable part of our community life. To my
astonishment, I now learned that she had never before worked
in a library or studied the subject. Like Mozart, who began compos-
ing symphonies at the age of five, Mrs. Wenck seemed to have
brought into this life the "knowing" of how a library should be
operated.*

*Returning to their narrative of that particular Egyptian period,
the Guides wrote:*

Arthur (Demorathage) visited you and your husband
several times in Heliopolis, and great was the feast of
knowledge spread lavishly around the table when others
came to speak with the eminent scholar and to test out new
ideas and inventions. You lived happily with your scrolls
and your dogs, and you had two young children. You
were scarcely thirty years old when that life ended through
the bite of an adder while you were walking in your seques-
tered garden beside the Nile, but such happiness and
knowledge were crammed into that life that it seemed complete and totally satisfactory to you after you passed to
spirit.

In that lifetime you made progress, since you were loving
and giving and enraptured with the knowledge that you
would leave for future generations. The material you compiled on the ancient continent of Atlantis was placed in
the archives of the library at Alexandria, but has since
been destroyed even as the library itself eventually disappeared. Your abiding interest in that subject explains why

you instantly believed in the existence of ancient Atlantis when you first came in contact with that revived knowledge in the present era.

You were by no means perfect in that life, as you were overproud of your learning and accustomed to having your own way as a cherished daughter and wife, but in all it was a progressive life and a worthwhile one. This Egyptian life began three centuries before the birth of the child in Bethlehem who altered the course of history. Atlantis had been gone but not yet forgotten in those ancient times, and Plato had written of it a century earlier in Greece, having learned from an Egyptian priest about those matters that were then fairly common knowledge among the educated class of Egypt.

Under hypnosis five years ago by the woman scientist whom I called Jane Winthrop in Here *and* Hereafter, *I seemingly relived the final day of that lifetime. In my mind's eye I still vividly see the garden and the sparkling waters of the Nile below, as I walked among rows of flowering plants. I was lyrically happy in that altered state of consciousness, while describing the garden, but when the hypnotist asked me to proceed to other happenings I could not do so. Finally I realized that I was no longer in the body, and when I told her I had died, she instructed me to look back and see what had happened.*

The tape recorder shows that I said, "Oh, I understand now! I stepped on a little adder. I didn't mean to, but I was wearing sandals and it must have bitten me."

The hypnotist asked me to continue watching the scene, and I exclaimed, "I see my husband's bowed head. Why, it's Hugh Lynn Cayce!" She asked if he were grieving, and I replied, "Yes, but he won't grieve for long. He's a good man. He will marry again." I felt brief sadness as I saw a baby and knew it to be mine, but then I seemed lost in eternity and could not return to the scene.

CHAPTER

19

Greece
(Fourth or Fifth Century A.D.)

The great seer Edgar Cayce taught that most of us, before completing our cycles of rebirth, must undergo life as both man and woman, dwell in every great geographical area, be a member of all five races, and experience all major religions. The Guides assert that I am always happier as a woman than a man, but they nevertheless related three widely separated incarnations in which I am said to have occupied the body of a male. The first was in the land of Moab, and the second was "as a young boy in Greece, after the time of Jesus by several centuries." Of this period they wrote:

You were a student in the school originally founded by Aristotle, but this was long after his time. It was not the Golden Age of Greek culture, but an Athenian one nevertheless, where learning was higher than in most other parts of the ancient world. Rome had of course conquered Greece, and thus you were a Roman citizen but of Greek descent.

Arthur Ford was then an instructor in the school, teaching philosophy and rhetoric, as speechmaking was then termed, and there you learned public speaking as well as the art of thinking through a subject to logical conclusions. You lived at the school during the youth of that life and were a good student, although not much interested in athletics, which was considered important then.

205

This was a time of much political change, but you were so far isolated from that subject that you dreamed only of restoring Greek culture in all its sublimity. You were a mere lad, but dedicated to the rule of God on earth, each person to be an individual helping all others to assert their rights through unfolding of learning and perfect oneness, not by political turmoil or overthrow of existing rule, but through enlightenment and culture. This, then, was your dream, and Arthur Ford was the teacher who fired your imagination with the glories that would come when all were free and truly equal in learning and understanding. A utopian dream, but one which you both had brought into that life from previous understanding.

Women held no interest for you except as equals among your peers, and for that brief life all seemed easy of attainment until rebels and invaders toppled the rule of one Caeophus, who had furthered the ideals of the Aristotelian school, and turmoil was unleashed upon that ancient land. Then the schools were closed and men forced into the fighting forces.

Arthur had encouraged you to devote your life to teaching, but in your twenty-first year you, who hated violence, fell from a horse in battle and died.

Since this is a period of Greek history about which I knew exactly nothing, I referred to an encyclopedia and learned that in the fourth century "the schools of Athens still retained much of their prestige." Farther along I read that the incursion of the Visigoths in 395–396 "was accompanied by a systematic devastation that crippled Greece for decades," and that Vandal pirates raided the country in the following century. The Guides did not say to which invasion I owed my demise, but having died once before at the hands of invaders, in the Persian incarnation, it seemed rather unfair.

I asked the Guides if there was any significance to that fact, and they replied: "You were paying back no particular karma in dying at the hands of raiders, because many such incursions occurred in those days and it was a common way of departing the body. Arthur [Ford] lived to a ripe old age, since he was of scholarly mien and posed no threat to conquering hordes." Then, taking their usual crack at me, the Guides wrote: "In that life you pursued learning, as you have ever done, being more often student that teacher. This is a fault, since you are taking rather than giving in that role."

Somewhat abashed, I asked if I had made any progress in that incarnation. "What did you learn?" they asked. "Goodness of heart and the futility of violence. Simply one of many, many lifetimes along the road toward final peace. So short and uneventful that not much else about it is of interest, as recorded in the akashic records."

In that event, it is not surprising that I have preferred my earthly stints as a woman. So much more seems to happen!

Tibet (Circa A.D. *850)*

There may have been more significance to that lifetime in Greece than the Guides earlier indicated, because at one point, while discussing my three "male" incarnations, they made this intriguing commentary: "In Moab it was the body which worked, in Greece it was the mind, and in Tibet the spirit." They had concluded their discussion of that dull life in Moab by writing, "In all, it was not a wasted life, but one of suspension." Now they began the story of the Tibetan period by remarking:

A life in the Himalayas was a similar time of resting for the soul, but at a much higher level than in Moab, for here you worked intensively at spiritual growth as a young guru who eventually succeeded your own guru, Arthur Ford. Both of you were trying to rid selves of worldly pursuits and think only on that which was sublime. This was an uplifting experience, although a soul should not too often devote itself solely to that which is not of the physical world, for many are the improvements for mankind that are to be accomplished within the framework of the working world.

It would not do for everyone to sit and contemplate his navel while reaching for self-perfection. An occasional such lifetime is beneficial, but the purpose of your life today is to reach as many as possible through introduction of the truths of eternal life and the importance of assisting others along the way, loving God and one's fellowman.

Meditation is important, yes, but not all day or all night. Better to have a skillful blending of being and doing.

I vaguely recalled that at some earlier time Arthur had warned against spending an entire life span in meditation or contemplation, as some Eastern religions encourage. He indicated that by removing ourselves from worldly temptations and devoting ourselves entirely to perfecting our own beings, we were losing the greater opportunity of helping others over the rough spots. Presumably this means that if we are thinking only of saving our [own] souls, we are in danger of losing them.

In the Tibetan life your father was a merchant in the town, and as was the custom, most small boys were instructed by wise men, or savants, until they were ready to go away to school. This happened with you, and you were drawn to the life of a guru, with its quietude and sense of universal vibration. When you returned to the village from school, you therefore entered the order and became a guru for small boys in the village while you simultaneously studied under Arthur Ford, who was then a higher guru in another ashram farther up the mountain.

The diet was nuts, fruits, roots, and legumes. You ate no meat and killed no living thing. Your greatest happiness was the days when you would trudge up the mountain to the higher ashram and sit in lotus position at the feet of your guru, who taught you to open your inner eye and sense the world of eternal spirit.

It is interesting to note that in my present lifetime I was a vegetarian until I married Bob, although my parents, brother, and sister were meat eaters who maintained a normal diet. I presume that I did also until the age of five, when after having fried chicken for dinner one Sunday, I wandered out to the back of the garden, where Mother kept a few chickens for the table.

I had noticed that one had a distinctive topknot, and when I rushed in to tell Mother that this particular chicken had disappeared, she explained that we had eaten it for dinner. I shall never forget my shock. From that day forward I refused to touch any food that had been killed, to the chagrin of family, relatives, and friends. But I lived quite happily on a diet consisting mainly of dried lima beans, peanut-butter sandwiches, vegetables, and apple sauce until the time came that I had to cook meat for Bob. Then, I began eating it.

Perhaps my prejudices suddenly changed at that time because of my particular karmic relationship with Bob. The Guides claim that he had been my husband in the Palestinian incarnation, when even Jesus ate meat. It is a possible explanation, which earlier I had been unable to comprehend.

To return to the Guides:

Strong were the ties that bound you and your guru. When Arthur Ford passed on, you anointed his body, and after the cremation you took his place as the guru in his ashram. This was in A.D. 867 in Tibet. That life was fruitful in soul growth, overcoming temptations of the flesh, and helping others to achieve mastery over self.

That was a lifetime of quiet meditation and devout adoration of the Creator, and when you finally passed out of the flesh, it was with a feeling of oneness with all creation. Neither you nor Arthur was a saint, but simply dedicated souls who wished to devote selves to teaching and adoration of the One God. You would return again and again to develop talents and assist others on the lonely path toward perfection, even as you then were striving for that glimpse of the eternal, but in some lives you were more successful at this goal than in others. Ever has there been inner awareness of the quest, however, and the need for surmounting the hurdles leading toward eventual reunion with God.

I asked for enlightenment on what Arthur Ford had taught

*me when he was my guru, and the Guides wrote: "How to project
self into the minds of others, subconscious communication with
others of God's creation such as bees, wasps, animals and birds,
inner stillness, mind projection, and astral travel without leaving
one's lotus position."*

Since I once had an alarming reaction from a wasp sting,
and I have been unable to experience astral travel, I asked the
Guides: "Then how did I lose this power to such an extent that
I can't even meditate effectively now?"

They replied with equanimity: "Why not relearn it now?
Relearning is always easier than original learning, and within
the soul that you are now is this earlier knowledge."

I asked how to go about relearning it, and with a jocular
air my spirit pen pals responded: "By the application of the seat
of the pants to the floor or a chair for extended periods of time,
while you still the thoughts and project self abroad in the land.
Practice communion with other creatures great and small, through
meditation and by reaching out to their vibrations."

Frankly, my heart has never been in it when I have occasionally
attempted astral travel during meditation. After a lifetime spent
as a newspaper reporter and columnist, which involves rather
too much snooping, I have no current desire to drop in on people—even in astral form—and look over their shoulders. The
Guides never fail to remark on my faults, which indicates that I
shall have to return to physical form many times more, so I think
I'll reserve that adventure for a subsequent incarnation.

Readers of A World Beyond may recall that under prenatal
hypnotic regression by the woman scientist I call Jane Winthrop,
I relived flashes of the Tibetan life six years ago. Even today
I "see" those two ashrams as vividly as I did then. As the scene
opened, I was sitting in lotus position at an ashram that I knew
was located in the lower Himalayas. I can still "see" my skinny
brown arms, and I identified myself as a young guru for small
boys who lived in the village below. Under questioning, I described
our diet of berries, fruits, and nuts, and I said that I personally

studied with a more advanced guru whose ashram was higher up the mountain.

After Jane Winthrop took me forward twenty-five years and asked if I were still in the ashram, I looked about in perplexity, until realization dawned that I had succeeded my deceased guru and was now in the higher ashram. When asked to give my mantra (said to be each soul's unique vibration with the universe), I burst forth in a cadence previously unknown to me, melding two syllables into one, time after time.

A few weeks later a stranger who introduced himself as Dr. I. C. Sharma of Udaipur, India, came to call. I had told no one of that experience under hypnosis, but when I expressed the wish to know my mantra, Dr. Sharma said that he would meditate on it. A week later he returned and handed me a slip of paper on which he had jotted the exact mantra I uttered for the benefit of Jane Winthrop. There is no possibility that the philosophy professor from India could have picked up those specific sounds in any normal way, since only Jane had heard them and she flew to the West Coast the morning after our session. She has never known Dr. Sharma.

21

Italy (1452–1498)

I now ask your indulgence while the Guides relate a particularly significant life span that was said to have been shared by Lily and Arthur Ford, but not by me. Readers of my previous books know that Lily has repeatedly refused to divulge his identity, and since publication of A Search for the Truth *I have received many letters asking whether Lily has yet told me who he used to be. My answer has had to be no.*

After the Guides began dictating the material for this book, they gave numerous examples of lives Arthur Ford and I are said to have shared, in order to illustrate Group Karma and my recurring involvement with him. But since it was obvious that Lily was playing an active role in divulging the material they "researched" in akashic records, I finally asked rather plaintively if there wasn't some lifetime in which I had known Lily.

Without hesitation the writing began, "Ruth, this is Lily, Art, and the Group. Lily in the fifteenth century was a writer of note who dwelt in Italy and wrote on philosophical subjects, but this was not when you knew him, for that was in an English life when you were his daughter." Then began a description of an English period that I have placed in chronological order at the end of this book.

At the beginning of the next day's session, being endowed with a large supply of curiosity and persistence, I asked for Lily's name when he was a writer in Italy, and to my astonishment they wrote, "He was Savonarola in the fifteenth century in Florence, and

*he published many of his sermons and governmental reforms as
well as philosophy, but some of these works have been destroyed.
Arthur Ford was also a Dominican priest at that time and aided
Lily in some of his proposals, for he too was on the side of freedom
and liberty. You were not then in physical embodiment."*

*Savonarola a priest? A Dominican? Readers may be shocked
by such an appalling gap in my knowledge, but except for recognizing the name, I knew exactly nothing about Savonarola. Had
I been asked on a quiz show to identify him, I would probably
have said that he was some sly politician like Machiavelli, whose
name has become synonymous with unscrupulous cunning. I certainly would not have guessed Savonarola was a monk, and if
told that he was, I most assuredly could not have named his order.
I also had no idea where Savonarola had lived, but because I
am always eager to check the accuracy of the Guides, I resisted
the temptation to look him up in reference books. At the next
session I therefore prodded the Guides for more information about
Lily's alleged life as Savonarola, and they wrote:*

Savonarola was highly esteemed by his peers and was
eager to establish equality among men, to the extent that
such a radical idea could be conceived in those difficult
times. He wanted the State to treat all men alike and to
establish a rule by law and not by the capricious fancy
of men in power. He was ahead of his times, and when
he acquired the enmity of those who wielded power for
selfish motives, his days were doomed, for he was as a
voice crying in the wilderness.

A good, good man who made rapid advances in his
spiritual development, so that he has been much loved
on this side of the door called death. He had succored
the helpless and given of himself to worthy pursuits, endur-
ing the scorn of his superiors with bravery and without
rancor. Later, in another incarnation, he became a noted
writer whose words lifted the hearts of many, as he sought
to justify the works of those who would aid the suffering,
but we will not tell you about that at this time. In his

lifetime as Savonarola he was above those who demeaned him and would have made an even greater impact on his times except that the Church denounced him, so that he fell from popularity and was martyred. But he kindled a few lamps, and his influence grew with the passage of time. He himself knew great suffering in that life in Florence.

I was undergoing a bit of mental suffering myself. I had a burning curiosity to know more about Savonarola, in order to challenge the Guides, but I managed to restrain myself for nearly a month before they reverted to the subject, writing:

Now as to Lily when he was Savonarola: a fiery, intense man filled with righteous ardor and an intense longing to return Florentines to the path of righteousness as well as to win freedom for their physical selves. A driving personality who believed anything possible if men would pull together for the common good. A fierce intolerance for greed and hatred for the manipulation of people. Arthur Ford was one of his assistants, equally dedicated to the equality of man and freedom for individual behavior and thought. Both were then Dominican priests.

This was a time of turmoil and turbulence for the common people as well as their leaders. The Church was manipulative and meddlesome, ruled by petty, ambitious men whom Savonarola (Lily) sought to redeem through morality and equitable thought. Savonarola (Lily) so antagonized those whom he sought to lead back to godly ways that he met death at the stake by burning; yet he kindled another flame that helped men lift themselves out of their mundane obsession with greed and selfishness. Arthur was also imprisoned, but eventually released. His name then was Prince Umberti and he was known as Father Gabrielli.

Savonarola was mystical; a sensitive who was aware of others' intentions and secret thoughts, but he was practical

in his application of the laws of God to man, desiring freedom and equality for all men and eager to direct them
inward to the search for God rather than outward to the
search for personal gain. Some considered him a fanatic,
and perhaps to an extent he was, in his burning zeal to
reform State and mankind, but so powerful was his message and his performance that he influenced the course
of history and rang a bell for liberty which is still to be
heard. A godly man who gave his life for those ideals that
knew no boundaries of nation or creed! Ford was an
intimate counselor and assistant who threw in his lot with
this man who had the power to lift mankind out of itself
to higher planes of wisdom.

*Since the Guides had said I was not incarnated during this
period of history, I decided that this offered sufficient "facts" to
check for accuracy. I therefore referred to the* Encyclopaedia
Britannica *and learned that Girolamo Savonarola, born to an
excellent family in 1452, scorned court life and entered a Dominican order, where he wrote poems of burning indignation against
the corruption of Church and court. A mystic, he had prophetic
visions that came true, and he seemed to read others' thoughts.
Lorenzo de' Medici, the ruler of Florence, sent for Savonarola
on his deathbed to receive absolution, but the Dominican friar
refused to grant it unless he "restored the liberties of Florence,"
and Lorenzo declined.*

*The encyclopedia further states that after the French invaded
Florence and then withdrew, Savonarola became the lawgiver
for that city, relieving the suffering of the starving and reducing
taxes on the lower classes. He "guarded the public weal with
extraordinary wisdom" and almost overnight changed pleasure-
loving Florence into an ascetic regime. Because he assailed the
corruption of the Vatican and Pope Alexander VI, the Borgia
who bought the papal throne, he was excommunicated and after
forty days of torture was given a mock trial. But he refused to*

recant his charges and bravely submitted to burning on a cross. He left behind an immense number of devotional and moral essays, numerous sermons, some poems, and a political treatise on the government of Florence.

This is but a brief capsule of Savonarola's career, to which the encyclopedia devotes many pages. Yet all that the Guides wrote about him proved to be accurate in every detail. Whether there was also a Father Gabrielli (Arthur Ford) with Savonarola at that time I do not know. But if Lily was indeed that martyred character of history, it could explain why he often exhibits such impatience with my own shortcomings. Such "burning zeal" for reform that some considered him a fanatic! Wow! No wonder I seldom seem to please him.

22

France
(Early Eighteenth Century)

Lily, having finally turned on the spigot of his past lives, seemed in no hurry to shut it off. For thirteen years I had tried without success to glean some hint of his identity. But who says thirteen is an unlucky number? After unburdening himself about the life in Italy which he and Arthur Ford allegedly shared as Dominican friars, he now permitted the disclosure of a French incarnation when he reportedly knew me, but not Arthur. The Guides, in discussing this era, indicated that I was a rather unimportant female member of an impecunious family, to whom Lily lent a helping hand. They began in this fashion:

In the time of Louis XV you were sometimes at court, although you lived in Chartres and were not of the nobility. When the time was ripe for marriage, you were taken to Versailles, so that you would meet someone appropriate to wed. Your father had some land but not a great deal of money, and since you were motherless, you were left in the care of a woman who would look after your best interests. The woman to whose watchfulness you were assigned is now your mother, and although at that time she held the standing of a minor noblewoman, she was beholden to the king for her livelihood because as the widow of an impecunious count she had no separate maintenance. Countess Beatrice was her name then, and you became her ward.

At the palace you tarried for a time and there met an aide-de-camp named De Broissy, who would later be called Lily. In his youth he had been a goatherd in Normandy, until his uncle's title descended to him and he was summoned to court to take his rank with other young nobles. There he met you and soon became your confidant, for although he was married he wished you to make a good match. He therefore introduced you to other young swains, and since you would have almost no dowry, he tried to find one with sufficient substance not to need a wealthy wife.

Eventually Lily looked with favor on one titled the Duc de Chambris, and although you were not particularly attracted to the young man, who seemed shallow and immature, you did not want to disappoint De Broissy (Lily). You therefore wed the young duke and bore him several children, but had little in common with him or with the lavish court life of which you were seldom a part, preferring to stay at home and read.

Later, while rereading this segment of Lily's mysterious correspondence, I was suddenly struck with the thought, "So that is why my male Guide had long ago selected the symbolic Lily, a feminine-sounding name, as his signature!" Not only does the lily suggest purity, but the fleur-de-lis (or lily flower) was also the distinctive symbol of the royal family of France. Perhaps my spirit friend was wearing a replica of that heraldic device when I knew him at Versailles, and he was trying to awaken my soul memory.

The Guides next introduced two friends of mine in the present era, Hope Ridings Miller of Washington, D.C., author of Embassy Row *and* Scandals in the Highest Office, *and Jean (Mrs. Robert) Birkin of Cuernavaca, writing:*

Hope Miller was in the French life with you and was well placed at court, although not of the royal family, as you were not. She shared your secrets and established herself in a secure position, so that often she went to the palace of Versailles to enlist favors from the king for less fortunate friends. Lily was friendly with her in that lifetime when her name was Louise, and yours was Marelle.

I could understand why my good friend Hope would have been more "highly placed" at the French court than I. Tactful, kindly, and popular, she is very much a part of the social whirl in Washington, loving the parties that are so numerous that I moved away from the nation's capital partly to escape those daily rounds. Hope is always up on the latest fashions, and once when we were chatting at a fashionable dinner dance, she helpfully remarked that wearing a wristwatch with evening dress was no longer in style. Glancing at my own wristwatch, I remember remarking, "But, Hope, I would so much rather know the time than to be fashionably dressed!" There was my worship of time again! Continuing the narrative, the Guides wrote:

You also knew Jean Birkin as another lady at court, a friend who helped with introductions to those who came for weekends of shooting. Although you did not participate in the hunts, the eligible young swains were there in force, and it was a time for getting acquainted. Jean was a lady-in-waiting to the queen, who although regally above all of you was not unkind, and was a frolicking companion when in the company of women, saving her arts for the king and other men.

This apparently referred to the days before the emergence of Madame de Pompadour as the king's favorite, since the encyclopedia, in discussing the earlier years of Louis XV, commented that "the queen [Maria Leszczynska] for some time seems to have secured his affections, and she bore him seven children." Addressing me directly, the Guides next wrote:

Your life in France was not a particularly happy one. The times were not given to deep devotion, but rather to frivolity, and your husband strayed many times from the home. Your children were much like him, seeking pleasures at court, and you were much alone because you did not care for the atmosphere of Versailles and for the courtesans who would fawn upon the emperor and the high born. Although an interesting life, it was not a particularly spiritual one. Rather, it was a struggle for you in the early years, and then with your growing family a time of watchful waiting and suspension.

Thus it was with some relief that at the age of forty-two you felt yourself approaching death, and you bore with pride the loneliness of your last weeks, slipping away in your bed while others slept. The disease was similar to what nowadays is called influenza.

Dead again! At a somewhat later date I asked the purpose of that incarnation, and the Guides responded: "That French life has a lesson for all of us in that, in the midst of frivolous pursuit of pleasure, there are those who seek the deeper meaning of living and simple pleasures of the heart. Those who in endless pursuit of frivolity and frenetic attempts to avoid boredom run hither and yon are wasting their time in physical embodiment." (Certainly neither Hope Miller nor Jean Birkin has frittered away her life, since both have made the most of their numerous talents and have accomplished much good. Interestingly, both prefer furniture of the Louis XV period to any other, as do I, and I have a sizable collection of French antiques.)

The Guides, pursuing the subject of wasted time, cautioned: "There is strong competition to return to human form, to undo previous errors and expand one's consciousness. When an incarnation is squandered in pursuit of fleshly indulgences, we have not only wasted our own opportunity but also have denied it to others in the spirit realm." This was a reference to competition in the spirit world for "available vehicles," as Arthur Ford terms pregnant women; and he said the matter is usually settled by "heavenly computers" that decide which soul can enter the body of a newborn baby.

Continuing their warning, the Guides wrote: "Take heed, then, of the squandered days and years, for as the downshift in the population spiral sets in, there will be fewer opportunities for all of you to return again soon. These upward waves of births, which governments have been calling a 'population explosion,' occur now and then, but such a one as this through which the earth has just passed has not been seen since Atlantean days when the land mass was greater, the civilization higher, and the land of Mu contained such overpopulation that many were exiled to less desirable areas for residence."

Edgar Cayce and other psychics have made reference to a lost continent of Mu, which is said to have occupied a large area off the North and South American west coasts in the Pacific Ocean. Cayce gave few details, because not many of those who came to him for readings seem to have had previous lives in Mu, but many of them were told of Atlantean incarnations. This would again seem to support the thesis that groups of souls who have known each other choose to return at the same time; then they step aside while other souls with different cycles of incarnation take their place in physical form.

I asked the Guides to elaborate on Mu, and they wrote: "Some dwelt in mounds beneath the soil, constructed as safety precautions to ease the danger from huge mammals that then walked the earth. The North Pole region in that age was tropical, so that there was an abundance of food and space for habitation there. A time will shortly come when the tropical areas of today will become frigid, and the earth will for a time be less habitable than now. It is therefore well for all who read these words to give thought to achieving such perfection now that they will not need to return to earth form for perhaps a millennium.

"With this in mind, we challenge the readers with this question: If you knew that you had only one more week in which to complete *your present embodiment, and no further opportunity for a thousand years to advance spiritually and draw closer to God, would you be wasting your time on frivolities, gossip, and attempts to outsmart business associates? If this were the last time to attempt perfection of soul, what a radical improvement there would be in all mankind! So why not attempt that program now? For a week give it the 'old school try.' Let nothing stir you to uncontrolled anger and nothing prevent you from helping others. Live for one week as if all future lifetimes depended on it, and see if this will become habit-forming. Discover how much better you feel, spiritually, mentally, and physically. Give it a try. That is all we are suggesting."*

The grim reminder that "the tropical areas of today will become frigid" apparently refers to the prediction made by Edgar Cayce, and reiterated by Arthur Ford in A World Beyond, that the earth will drastically shift on its axis before the end of this century. Inasmuch as many modern geologists believe such a violent shift has occurred at least twice before, in prehistoric times, it is a sobering thought.

I have by now grown familiar with Lily's habit of moralizing, and since he too claimed to have been at the frivolous French court, I asked how he fared in that life. With due solemnity, the Guides replied: "Having proved his capacity for great good and self-sacrifice as Savonarola, he was in the French incarnation a likable, friendly man, quick to help others and smooth their path, while himself enjoying some of the fruits of his labors in Florence. A time of resting for a noble soul."

23

England (1806–1861)

It is with real trepidation that I approach a discussion of this final past life—if such it was. To assert soul-kinship with a Palestinian Ruth who knew Jesus is one thing, because there is no proof positive that she actually existed, but to lay claim to soul-sharing with a real-life woman of English letters is quite another. For this reason, until now I have studiously avoided any reference to the possible relationship. (I can hear the critics exclaiming, "Ye gods, look who she thinks she is now!") But my editor has perhaps overpersuaded me to include this peculiar set of circumstances in the anthology of my alleged lives.

In late February, 1968, while gathering material for a book about reincarnation *(Here and Hereafter),* I heard of a youth named Robert Morrison who seemed to some a reincarnation of King Tutankhamen. An acquaintance supplied the telephone number of his mother, Mrs. Roberta Mueller, and when I explained the purpose of my call she agreed to bring her son to our house in Virginia Beach. It was an interesting session, during which I heard tapes of a life reading the lad once had with a woman psychic. Then, with their acquiescence, I arranged for him to be prenatally hypnotically regressed at my house the following week.

On first meeting we had discussed his vivid dreams about

apparent past lives. Now, when they arrived for the second visit, his mother exclaimed, "Bobby had a dream about you and Mr. Montgomery the other night, about when he knew you in a previous lifetime. But all I'll tell you is that you were a rather well-known English couple in the nineteenth century."

Without conscious thought, I blurted, "Don't tell me we were the Brownings." She clapped her hand over her mouth, and I, as startled as she, laughed with mortification at my unexpected words.

"Tell her your dream," Mrs. Mueller prompted. Her son responded, "Well, I saw a man in a flowing robe whom I've seen before in my dreams—often enough to recognize that when he speaks I must listen and remember. [Edgar Cayce taught that such a figure is the dreamer's higher self, or superconscious.] This dream figure told me that you and Mr. Montgomery were Elizabeth and Robert Browning in your last lifetime, and that I was associated with you in some way. I didn't know anything about them, so I looked up the Brownings in the school library before we came over today. They were poets."

While I cringed with embarrassment, Mrs. Mueller took up the thread, saying earnestly, "Not only that, but after Bobby told me his dream at breakfast, I dreamed that night that you were indeed the Brownings. Then I found a picture of Robert Browning in a library book. It looks almost like your husband, Robert. Now, don't tell me your middle name is Elizabeth, or it's just too much."

I weakly replied that after my birth Mother settled on the name of Elizabeth for me, until Dad raised such a storm of protest that they agreed to settle for Ruth. "But this is ridiculous. . . ."

Raising a hand to stop my protest, Mrs. Mueller continued, "Wait, there's more. You know Mrs. [blank] who is psychic? I called to tell her Bobby had dreamed about your past life, and before I could say another word she exclaimed, "Don't tell me . . . I'm getting it . . . she and her husband were the Brownings."

"Mental telepathy." I laughed, dismissing the subject.

A few days later Mrs. Mueller telephoned, her voice vibrating with excitement. "Listen to this," she began, "and I swear every word of it is true. Today in the supermarket I saw a cousin of Hugh Lynn Cayce's for the first time in months, and she rushed over to tell me that she simply has to go to Washington because she wants to meet Ruth Montgomery. I asked why and she said, 'Because as I was coming down the stairs this morning, it was as if a voice spoke to me out of nowhere saying that Ruth was Elizabeth Barrett Browning. I feel I must tell her about it.' I said you were now living right here in Virginia Beach, and at first she wouldn't believe me, but how do you like that for proof?"

I scoffed that there must be a lot of ESP flapping around Virginia Beach, but after Hugh Lynn's cousin (whom I had not previously met) verified her experience to me, I did admit to a few coincidences. For instance, from earliest childhood I was writing verse, and at Baylor University (which is known as the Poet's College) I majored in poetry. My guiding light there was Dr. A. Joseph Armstrong, head of the English department, who had amassed for Baylor University the largest Browning collection in the world.

I could not recall having entertained any particular interest in Elizabeth B. Browning, but when I mentioned these coincidences to my younger sister, Margaret Overbeck, she exclaimed, "No particular interest! Why, don't you remember that when I was a child you used to sit me down in a chair and make me listen by the hour while you read Elizabeth Barrett Browning's sonnets to me? All I've ever known about her poetry is what you told me then, but I can still recite some of it by heart."

I vaguely recalled that E.B.B. had been an invalid, but not until my curiosity was piqued by Bob Morrison and

I bought a book about her did I realize she had suffered from a mysterious back ailment which kept her confined to her couch throughout much of her life. I have often since 1960 been plagued by such painful muscular spasms in my back that I've been in and out of hospitals and on and off osteopathic couches, although no one located the cause.

E.B.B's biographers tell of her distinct preference for the color green, which was mine in childhood; of her love for her adopted Italy, which has ever been my second love; and of her overriding interest in politics, as mine has been since the quarter-century I spent as a syndicated political columnist in Washington, D.C. Elizabeth was "always in a hurry," as I have been. She, like I, had greater rapport with her father than her mother. And to my astonishment I learned that after her marriage E.B.B. developed a deep interest in psychic phenomena and communication with the so-called dead, despite her husband's occasional disapproval and total disinterest. This too has happened to me.

Even her addiction to opium provides food for thought. In nineteenth-century England, when opium's addictive qualities were yet unknown, it could be bought freely in pharmacies, and Elizabeth's doctors invariably prescribed it for her pain. I have always adored the taste of paregoric, and until I learned that it contained opium I used to remark, "If this weren't so constipating, I could happily drink a quart of it." In this life I have assiduously avoided drugs or any type of painkillers, fearful of developing the habit, although doctors have always recommended them for my back pains. Yet I confess to a lamentable zest for cigarettes, and in *A World Beyond* Arthur Ford warned that unless one overcomes habit-forming pleasures in one life he is likely to return with "an unnatural craving" for some other indulgence in the next lifetime.

Certainly I bear no physical resemblance to Elizabeth

Barrett Browning, although biographers have written of her "exquisite hands and feet," and those extremities of mine have also been much admired by friends, strangers, and even an Egyptian ambassador whom we met at a dance.

Until Elizabeth met and married Robert Browning at the age of thirty-nine, the greatest love of her life had been her brother Edward (Bro), who died by drowning in early manhood. Her other favorite was their possessive father, Edward Barrett Moulton Barrett. The Guides now identify Arthur Ford as Bro and Lily as the father. They also attribute E.B.B.'s back trouble, as well as mine, to the Egyptian life (circa 1300 B.C.) in which "we" were shoved off a promontory. During the period that Arthur Ford was communicating the material for *A World Beyond* and answering my questions about what had happened to various famous people, I asked, "What is Elizabeth Barrett Browning doing now?" To which he promptly replied, "You should know. She's sitting at this typewriter asking me questions."

Here, then, is the story Lily, Arthur, and the Guides have dictated at various times during a period of four months. But remember, I can't "prove" a word of it.

"In the early decades of the nineteenth century you and Arthur Ford were children together in a large household. His name was Edward and you were Elizabeth. He was your brother, and the two of you were nearly inseparable both in activities and thought. Each had a well-nigh brilliant mind, quick to learn and to do. Once, many years earlier, your father surprised you as you were telling Edward about a previous life in which you remembered being an Egyptian princess, and the boy excitedly recalled his life then as a pharaoh. Fortunately for you children your father in that English life thought you were imagining the story, as so many children do, and did not rebuke you for telling falsehoods, thereby shutting off your faint awareness of previous lives.

"Then one day you fell from a pony, and although you did not seem seriously injured, the back trouble you had suffered in that previous Egyptian life entered your consciousness, and from that time on the back seriously bothered you even unto your death. Now in this present life you still trail that remembrance, albeit subconsciously, of the Egyptian period, so let us tell you about that in order to free you from clinging veils that keep you entrapped. As a princess in Egypt around 1300 B.C., the tradition existed that a woman pharaoh was bad luck. . . ." The Guides then introduced the story of that ancient Egyptian lifetime, which I have previously recounted in this book, when a bribed servant allegedly shoved me from a promontory.

The above writing occurred on April 10, 1973, and each morning thereafter the Guides dictated material on other lifetimes that Arthur Ford and I have allegedly shared. At last, wearying of Lily's strange reticence about his own identity in earth lives, I began the May 15 session by asking if I had been acquainted with Lily in some previous embodiment. To my surprise, Lily readily wrote: "Yes, that was in Britain and not so long ago. You were born to parents whose money stemmed from slave labor in Jamaica. The oldest of a large brood of children, you were the family favorite, and Arthur Ford, the second child, named Edward, was also adored by the father. I was that father."

Excitedly I asked, "Is this when you were a famous writer?"

"Not in that life," he replied, "for in this one of which I now speak I encouraged *your* ability to write both poetry and philosophy and to use your fluency in languages to translate the ancient Greek and other philosophers. You were a comely child, slim and dark-haired, with dainty hands and feet, and you loved to romp with Edward and the younger children until you fell from a pony one day, bringing back such soul memories of your tortured broken back in Egypt that this deeply settled into your emotional system. Thereafter you were a partial cripple, although the doctors and specialists whom I brought to you could find nothing basically wrong.

"I felt, with you, that there was a real injury, for I did not then know of your soul memories from ages past. I therefore pampered you too much, whereas had I not loved you so deeply, I would have ordered you to ignore the back and get on about the joy of living. You and I had been together happily in other lives, and for this reason I automatically adored you to a greater extent than the younger children, which was unfair but overpowering."

Until the next paragraph I was not sure of the intended identity. Then Lily wrote: "The story is well known of the courtship of you by Robert Browning, and of my initial approval of his visits to your sickroom, for I had subconsciously encouraged you to be an invalid, feeling this would keep you ever in my home. When you eloped, I was so crushed that the life went out of me, for my particular world had ended. To be repelled and repulsed by the one object of my adoration was too much, and my spirit was broken. Forgiveness? I scarcely knew the meaning of the word. The wound was too deep, and for this I have been paying time out of mind. To love is divine, yes, but to love with such possessiveness as I had done is a sin against our Father, for we truly love only when we gladly surrender our needs for another's happiness. This folly of mine, this sin of great depth has tortured me since, and for this reason when I took over at your typewriter in this life I was determined to free you whenever you desired it. Sometimes I have been too domineering even now, and often too demanding, and for this I continue to pay. The struggle to overcome it has been real and strong and tortuous."

Then the writing stopped, and after reading it I felt such shock that I demanded, "Lily, is this true or does it stem from my subconscious?"

"Why would it come from your subconscious?" he countered. "Had you ever thought of my being your father before?"

Certainly I had not, but after a moment I pressed. "If it's true that you were that possessive father, how could you now appear as a shining white light to Mrs. Olga Worrall *(Here and Hereafter)* and to Arthur Ford *(A World Beyond)*? How would you so quickly have overcome that karma and become a highly developed soul?"

"Think it through," he replied. "One step backward does not destroy the total attainments of many previous lives, and I have truly repented of this sin. We are the sum of our Total Being throughout eternity. Sometime I will tell you more."

So *that* was why Lily, in the early years of our mysterious correspondence, had occasionally seemed so domineering! From the beginning of our relationship I had sensed that he was high-minded and spiritual, having only my good at heart; yet I was often puzzled by his bossiness and apparent irritation when I failed to do as he instructed. When he ordered me to buy the house that he had eerily located for me on Sheridan Circle in Washington *(A Search for the Truth)*, I did not do so until I personally decided that it would bring happiness. Sometimes I overslept, thus missing our early-morning sessions at the typewriter, and Lily was not amused. He loathed my cigarette smoking and was impatient of my frailties. What a contrast he was to Arthur Ford, who after his death became a witty and understanding companion at the morning sessions. So *this* was why! Yet how deeply interested in my spiritual progress Lily had always been, how uplifting his thoughts, and how obvious his devotion! It seemed a revelation.

In the days that followed, Lily gave me glimpses of his alleged life as Savonarola, but on May 19 the Guides wrote: "That was not when you knew him, for this was in the English life when you were Elizabeth Barrett and he was your father. That abiding love he felt for you then has carried over, and he has deeply regretted the hardness of his heart when you married the man you loved enough to desert hearth and home. He realizes that had he opened his heart to Robert Browning, there would have been no need for you to leave the house in secrecy and he would then have enjoyed the devotion and esteem of daughter and son-in-law alike. Thus he has had many regrets and has not since reincarnated, but has worked strenuously here to overcome that blot on an otherwise good escutcheon."

"But," I countered, "I still don't see how Lily could seem as a bright, highly evolved soul if he had slaves in those days and treated his children as he did, forbidding them to marry and demanding complete obedience."

"Because," they responded, "he had risen to high peaks in previous lives, and fell only because he loved so much that he also wished to possess. This was the error, and he has been working steadfastly here to overcome it."

Another day the writing began: "Your lifetime as E.B.B. is such an informative one that we will provide more information. You were a mischievous, loving little girl who worshiped your father [Lily] and the eldest of your younger brothers, Bro [Arthur Ford]. The other children also were adored by you, although to a lesser degree, and your mother was a sweet person, although she lacked your brilliant mind. Languages came easily to you in that life, and with Lily's encouragement you soon knew them well enough to translate from ancient Latin, Greek, and Hebrew. This was a carryover from your Palestinian life, though there had been many lives between those two. You have shown no reluctance to return repeatedly to physical body, for you have a zest for living that is pleasing to the gods who watch over us.

"In that life Lily felt such pride in you and such deep-seated affection that it seemed impossible for him not to feel overly possessive, and for this he has paid. When you were a child, he had dreams of your becoming a writer of renown, and as you turned to poetry, his enthusiasm knew no bounds. This was the exemplification of that which he had wished for himself at an earlier age. (He also wrote poetry as Savonarola.) For this reason the father's encouragement kept you chained to your pencil and paper to please him whom you loved, even when inspiration was often lacking. The back problem stemmed, as we have said, from that soul memory of an earlier life in Egypt.

"When you met Robert Browning, you recognized a deep-seated attraction carried over from previous lives when you had known him well (he was Jonathan, Ruth's husband in the Palestinian life), and it was inevitable that you who had become an invalid more from emotional than physical causes should wish to be with him. Browning's will was then stronger than yours, and it was not difficult for you to agree to flee with him, since your father [Lily] would never have given consent to your leaving his household. However, he would have admitted Browning into that household as your mate, if properly approached, so it was wrong that you should deceive him and keep him uninformed of your romance.

"Lily would have resented that affection while he was embodied as Edward Barrett, but to keep you happy he would have permitted Browning to live within the walls of the house. [I wonder if Lily was now rationalizing his actions by means of hindsight.] Yet you were not to blame for wanting to try your own wings, which is the right of all those in physical form; so the impasse occurred, and the wrench persisted until Lily at last was able to make contact with you through this type of writing. Thus, with this link now established he is progressing rapidly here and feeling a song in his heart for having in some way helped to compensate for the unhappiness he caused you during his lifetime as Mr. Barrett."

Weeks later it occurred to me to ask, "Didn't Mr. Barrett and Elizabeth meet between lives to heal the wounds?" And they replied: "That they did, but as we regard time here, it was as a flash of lightning until Elizabeth returned to the physical world as you. A hundred years here is as naught, and fifty years is a twinkling of the eye. Reunited, yes, but although each forgave the other there was still the task of forgiving themselves and paying penance. This continues even unto this day."

Another morning Lily wrote: "At this time we would tell you about the life when we were all together in England as the Barretts. We were an extraordinarily close-knit family, having known each other in many previous lives, and all of us were devoted to learning and to truth. Your mother too had been friend and relative in some previous lives, but she was not so aptly attuned as the three of us: Myself, Arthur, and you. The other children who arrived after Elizabeth and Edward were also known to us from former times, but were less devoted to the principles of study than we were. Such devotion and adoration will always call for a high order of truth, and for the first half of that life together we were so involved with one another that we needed few outside contacts. Always there was the hearth and the home to satisfy our wants, and until Bro [Arthur Ford] died in a boating accident our calm was relatively unbroken."

The Guides then took over, writing: "Lily blamed Elizabeth for Bro's death, since she had defied his wishes by persuading Bro to stay with her at the resort where she was recuperating; and you were not without blame, for you were self-centered then as always. But it was intended to be, because Bro had fulfilled his pledge for that life, which was to unite in loving family circle and show himself worthy of devotion and ideals. There are few accidents in this world, if any, and his death was preordained by his own soul before entry into that body: to give up that which he loved above all else for karmic reasons, having become aware between lives that in the earlier Egyptian life he had caused (although unwittingly) the loss of your own life at an early age. We do have free will in the sense of conducting ourselves toward others as we would have them do to us, and are not therefore tools of some evil force which compels us to take the life of another.

"Judas Iscariot was not forced by something outside himself to betray the Master. He it was who made that choice, hoping to be elevated to a place of power within the Sanhedrin (rather than wanting the thirty pieces of silver). It was the lust for power which drove him to that evil task, and because it had already stamped itself on his intention Jesus was able to read it in his aura and know that he would do the deed."

In discussing Elizabeth Barrett's childhood, Lily declared that during her period of unconsciousness after the fall from the pony she glimpsed the Egyptian lifetime, when Arthur Ford had also been her younger brother and she had suffered the broken back that led to her death.

"Unfortunately," he continued, "the soul memory of it dragged down your condition and magnified the difficulty, whereas if you [Elizabeth] could have surfaced that past-life memory, you would have recognized the condition and conquered it. Thus, as you grew older, the subconscious memory haunted you to the extent that the back gave more and more trouble, and despite efforts of doctors it grew worse until you indulged yourself in invalidism. Could I have remembered for you or could Arthur have done so, it would have been understood by you, for you were much interested in the occult in that life as Elizabeth and should not have been surprised to hear of previous lives. After all, as a tiny child you'd had flashes of it. But neither of us then had the ability to recall past lives or to read the akashic records psychically."

In late July, while working on the material for this book,

I fell on my back and suffered such pain that I could not approach my typewriter for more than a week. The fall revived the muscular spasms that had so beleaguered me in Washington, but when I was able to return to my desk, the Guides referred immediately to the alleged English life, writing: "That lifetime as Elizabeth has more to it than you realize, for her fall from a pony brought back the soul memory of the Egyptian life and overshadowed that one. Therefore, do not let the back spasms get you down now, but continue on your regular round of activities and do not become housebound as you did in the Browning life. After Elizabeth gave way to that original despair she became a housebound invalid, and although it produced creative activity she would have been a greater poet to have gone out into the world and met the problems at first hand, as Robert Browning did, rather than read and hear of the travails of that era." (Surprisingly, the spasms quickly vanished.)

Reviewing the relationships of that lifetime, the Guides continued: "Even though the father [Lily] bitterly turned against E.B.B. through resentment and jealousy when she defied him by eloping, yet the love remained; and the remainder of her life was marred by her father's disavowal, just as his life was ruined by his own resentment. He has paid for that on this side with such overwhelming regret that when the opportunity to contact you came in 1960, he readily responded in order to atone for that injustice to you in the nineteenth century.

"You wonder how he could be as a shining light to us on this side when he was such an inconsiderate man as Mr. Barrett. The answer: because he has so devoted himself to compassion and understanding since coming over here and had otherwise lived such bountiful, generous lives in earlier incarnations that he was able to surmount that one regression of spirit. Edgar Cayce also had to overcome his wastrel life in Fort Dearborn (a previous incarnation during the Colonial period), which was a setback to his own growth, remember? This often happens as we spiral generally upward but sometimes become entangled in a net of our own wrongdoing. Elizabeth superseded love of father with love of husband, which was normal, but she was not without fault in neglecting to alert her father to this and discuss it with him rationally. Deceit is never the highest form of soul growth."

A few days later, without my request, Arthur Ford took command of the typewriter to declare that Elizabeth Barrett's sisters in that lifetime are now known to me. He said that actress Lisa Ferraday (Mrs. John W. Anderson II of Grosse Pointe, Michigan) was Henrietta and my present sister, Margaret, was Arabel. Taken completely by surprise, I had to consult reference books to determine that Henrietta and Arabel were indeed the names of E.B.B.'s two sisters. My sister, Margaret, and I seem perennially to be turning up in each other's lives, but Lisa? I had seen her no more than a half-dozen times, and then only briefly; yet we had experienced such instant rapport that she was now insisting on turning over to Bob and me her London flat, upon learning that we plan to spend the Christmas season in England.

Arthur Ford, after divulging that bit of information about the sisters, continued: "I was Bro and Lily was 'Edward the *père*.' Lily feels that reports of his obsessive possession are exaggerated in accounts you have read of that period, for although he is not proud of his behavior, he felt at the time that he was charged with a sacred duty to support his children and keep them together as a unit. It may be difficult for some to understand that in a way this was a fact, for members of our Barrett household had sworn to come back as a unit and remain dedicated one to another. Do you see what this means? In some sensitive way Lily recognized this obligation to help each child fulfill his prenatal pledge, but after meeting Robert

Browning, you felt an even stronger tie to an earlier pledge you had made to unite your life with his. The family pledge was the weaker of the two, for you had known the soul called Browning in many previous lives, including Palestine, and because the mating instinct supersedes family ties, it proved to be the irresistible one."

The Guides then wrote: "Elizabeth would have been wise to discuss this frankly with her father and tell him of her inner compulsions, for although she would have had to fight for her right, nonetheless it would eventually have dissolved the bitterness in his heart. Lily would have liked Browning, as he had liked him between lives. Thus it was your ego-self which blocked the way, as it repeatedly does in the soul entity to whom we are addressing this message. Try, try, Ruth, to put others before self. Dissolve the overweening ego which eternally blocks one's progress in the upward spiral, for although Lily was certainly at fault in that life, *you* were not blameless.

"He regrets it and has had to work on that particular possessive quality for a long time now. He will progress even more rapidly now that it is dissolving, and to do so he is helping you in this particular phase to free your own bonds by putting others before self. Lily had, after all, been Savonarola, and as a high prelate of the Church was not inured to being head of an active household of children or even to the duties of a husband. Coupled with the narrow virtues set by the Victorian age, it molded his character to stern steel, and it was perhaps unfortunate that he returned to flesh in that particular era, when the master of the house was master indeed!

"Yet, would Elizabeth Barrett have been so famed had it not been for the father who encouraged her from babyhood to devote herself to the Muses? Would the Browning love story reign eternal if Lily had gladly acquiesced the moment that a likely spouse was found for his invalid daughter? It was not he who made you an invalid but you yourself, still subconsciously remembering the injured back from Egypt, which was doubly brought to mind because it was Bro [*Arthur*], who had innocently been the cause of the fatal shove from the promontory above the Nile. In England the two of you had again returned as brother and sister. Again the devotion and the slight difference in age, with Arthur the younger of the two first-born children."

Rereading these passages troubled me more than I cared to admit. They interfered with my sleep and plagued my dreams. I did not want to include this alleged lifetime in a book addressed to the public, because I am acutely aware of the scoffers who jibe, "Why is it that everyone who believes in reincarnation claims to have been someone important? Whatever happened to the poor folks?" And I agree with that criticism. The Guides have indeed told me about some lives when I was appallingly inconsequential, including one when I was said to have been a black washerwoman in Africa; and under hypnosis I seemed to relive two dreary incarnations, one as a querulous, disagreeable farmer in Austria and another as a bored and boring German spinster. But I have not included them here because the Guides say I did not know Arthur or Lily in those lives, and this book is about Group Karma.

Another perturbing facet of the alleged life as E.B.B. has been the assertion by the Guides and the Virginia Beach psychics that my present husband was formerly Robert Browning. It is true that Bob Montgomery has always been able to quote long reams of poetry learned in his youth, and that he bears some physical resemblance to Browning's pictures and shares his sweetness of temperament. It is also true that several years ago, when I could not recall the name of Elizabeth Barrett Browning's dog, Bob instantly declared, "Flush." Yet in this life he chose management engineering as a career, and has evinced so little interest in classical literature that I stoutly challenged the

Guides, who replied: "Yes, Robert Montgomery was indeed Robert Browning. But he had exhausted his interest in writing poetry, having risen to the heights of his talent in that field, so he came back in this life to applaud the efforts of others and live quietly. Remember, we earlier described that cycle to you: the souls who may alternate in various lives between the pursuit of fame and artistic development, with the relaxing thereof."

Reverting then to the earlier subject matter, they continued: "Lily regrets deeply his position about marriage for his children, but his love for them was too encompassing, feeling as he did that they were his property. This was a throwback to his days as a Catholic prelate, when marriage was regarded by the Church as an inferior state, and he himself was denied marriage. Arthur Ford died early in that English life to escape the loss of freedom, for he innately knew that further sonhood with Mr. Barrett would lead to strong clashes of will and impossible hurdles. Thus his soul withdrew from that body at the height of young manhood. This happens with souls who are sufficiently advanced to know when it is best to retire, and he had come back in that life chiefly to be with Elizabeth and ease her path—a recompense for the Egyptian life when he had inadvertently taken her position on the throne."

How strange, if true, that my present life should be so powerfully influenced by the one immediately preceding it! And how odd that at least five alleged relatives in the Browning period should again be playing prominent roles in this life. Wondering whether there are others whom I knew then, my thoughts flashed to Dr. A. J. Armstrong, the beloved professor whose boundless enthusiasm for Robert Browning had driven him to amass the world's largest collection of Browningiana at a Baptist university in central Texas.

Of all the teachers and professors I have known and

loved, none exerted as much influence on my life as the head of the English department at Baylor; yet I did not know why. After all, I took two or more courses with numerous other professors, but only one with Dr. Armstrong. I had anticipated taking his Browning course during my senior year of college, but when Dad's business moved us north at the close of my junior year, shaky finances prevented my returning to Baylor, and I did not get to study Browning. Thus, although Modern Poetry was the only course I had with Dr. Armstrong, his personality was indelibly imprinted on my memory. He was a formidable teacher, so intent on bringing out the best in his students that they often trembled when he addressed them with displeasure. One day he instructed me to remain after class, and I thought I was in for it. The senior whom I was regularly dating promised to wait for me outside, and when Dr. Armstrong and I were alone, he abruptly demanded, "Are you going to marry that young man?" Unnerved, I stammered that I hadn't thought about it, to which he retorted, "Well, don't! You are going places in this world, and he isn't." With that he dismissed me, but he continued to take an unfailing interest in my progress, and after I left Baylor we commenced a correspondence that continued until his death.

I treasure one particular letter dated "3 A.M." when, unable to sleep, Dr. Armstrong was reading *Time* magazine and ran across a lengthy article about me in the press section. Reaching for pen and stationery, he promptly wrote to me in Washington, D.C., to express his "pride" in my development. I saw him only once more. While traveling through the South with the Eisenhower campaign train in 1952, I stayed over for a day in Waco to visit with Dr. Armstrong at the beautiful new Armstrong-Browning Building, which houses his Browningiana, a collection that has attracted scholars from all parts of the world.

Thinking on these incidents and many more, I asked

the Guides if Dr. Armstrong had perchance known the Brownings in a previous lifetime, and they wrote: "Dr. Armstrong is here and would have a word with you."

The pressure on the typing keys altered, and the writing began again: "Ruth I'm proud of the way you've developed and have had the courage to face down your adversaries and do that in which you believe, for it is truth that shines forth in your aura. I knew you in the Browning life, knew you and Arthur [Ford] when the Barretts still lived at Hope End, because I was a relative. By the time you moved to London I had already met the young Browning and become fascinated by his torrential talent. So few understood in those times the burst of power which emanated from him and the deep fastness of his being. I was Kenyon, and because of my admiration for the two of you I sensed the fires that would be kindled when you became acquainted. It was my pleasure to help with that courtship, but more, with the richness of merging two such divergent personalities into the one which crystallized in the brilliance of the union. At Baylor you were so outstanding that I recognized the need for you to find another such character as that of Browning, and when you eventually met him in your present life, although I was not then aware of identities, I felt that all was well. I am glad for you and send you my love."

Reading those lines afterward, it struck me as rather fanciful that a straitlaced man like the Dr. Armstrong I had known, who taught a Bible class at Waco's Southern Baptist Church throughout his years at Baylor, should be writing to me about reincarnation after his death. Somehow it seemed too out of character. But the thought of him evoked such nostalgia that I found a biography of him that was written twenty-two years ago. To my astonishment, I learned that he had been deeply interested in what his biographer called "transmigration of souls," but should probably have written "reincarnation." Naturally he would

have refrained from mentioning such an offbeat interest
to his students at a Baptist college in the 1930's and 1940's,
but here is a tantalizing paragraph from his authorized
biography by Lois Smith Douglas, called *Through Heaven's
Back Door:*

"The days of Lazarus before Christ raised him from
the dead have held a strong fascination for Dr. Armstrong.
Likewise has he shown much interest in men who believed in the transmigration of the soul—Khalil Gibran,
Tagore, and A. E. (George Russell). As full as has been
his own religious experience, he seems almost to express a regret that he has not shared one of those experiences."

The entity claiming to be Dr. Armstrong had written
on my typewriter, "I was Kenyon." This specific allusion
sent me again to reference books, where I learned that
John Kenyon was a distant cousin of Elizabeth Barrett
Browning's father and a devoted friend of Robert Browning. After the Barretts moved to London, Kenyon came
often to call on Elizabeth in her invalid's sanctum, and
it was he who encouraged a meeting between Robert and
Elizabeth. Kenyon delighted in their subsequent marriage,
and in his will he left the couple eleven thousand pounds,
much to the annoyance of the unrelenting Mr. Barrett.

Kenyon, a patron of the arts, was a collector of poets,
and he entertained them lavishly in his London home.
Dr. Armstrong brought so many outstanding poets as lecturers to Baylor that it became known as the Poet's College,
and they invariably stayed at his home rather than at a
hotel. Kenyon was a good friend of Walter Savage Landor,
and it was intriguing to learn in the biography of Dr. Armstrong that before settling his interest on Browning, he
had been an ardent fan of Landor's, writing a thesis about
his work and eventually securing his letters to Browning
for Baylor's collection.

But would it have been possible for John Kenyon to

reincarnate as A. Joseph Armstrong, since the latter was an elderly man when I first knew him? In an old *Who's Who in America* I found that Dr. Armstrong's birthdate was March 29, 1873. Yes, it was possible, since John Kenyon died December 3, 1856, and both men had devoted their lives to promoting others' poetry.

Tantalized by another reference in Mrs. Douglas' biography, I asked the Guides why Dr. Armstrong had been so interested in the life of Lazarus that his official biographer chose to comment on it while he was still living. They replied: "He was active in the Palestinian life, for he was a cousin of Lazarus and therefore also of yours, as he was in the Browning life. He lived in Bethany and spent much time with Lazarus, not only in learning to keep accounts and run an estate under Arthur Ford's tutelage but also in long hours of conversation and philosophy. He was so devoted to Lazarus and so bereaved by his death that when Jesus called forth Lazarus from the tomb, he became an ardent worshiper of Jesus. A good man and true, he gave up all to follow Him. Of course Dr. Armstrong believed in reincarnation, for often did it touch his sleeve when he recognized students whom he had known before; yet because of the narrow religious life at Baylor at that time he dared only occasionally hint at it. He loves you well and sends his blessing."

The Guides then terminated their discussion of the E.B.B. embodiment with these words: "The Browning life projected onto this one gives a pattern, if you will but see it. Love of writing, love of self, love of others who see as self sees, delight in recognition by others, and like-mindedness. Are you seeing it now? Still the same soul on its long quest for the Holy Grail, meeting self over and over on the long road toward expansion of consciousness and eventual reunion with the Universal Consciousness of God. Fellow travelers along the way, ever and again confronting those who have thwarted or assisted us at every turn of the long road. Lily the adoring father who thought he was helping, only to be a millstone around the neck of those he most loved. Arthur ever around to lend a step up, but sometimes proving to be a load to carry along. All of us striving to achieve that which was meant to be, but confronting ego and falling behind. The road is ever upward, but the path sometimes turns backward for a time. Never fear! Each life presents some gain, and the general trend is up, up, up. This is all for now. Love from us here."

As time passed, I found myself in odd moments becoming increasingly critical of Elizabeth and Robert Browning. The world adorns them with romantic trappings, idealizing them as hero and heroine in one of the "greatest love stories" of recorded history. But why? Perhaps Lily has handed me too many tools for self-examination, but it seems to me in the cold light of reasoning that their activities fell short of being "heroic."

To view them from a disinterested standpoint: Elizabeth, an invalid who was petted, indulged, and adored by her father, fell in love with a romantic young poet who worshiped at her couch. Risking the chance of bringing down her father's wrath on her younger brothers and sisters as well as herself, she surreptitiously permitted Robert to call in the afternoons when Mr. Barrett was out on business. Then, breaking forth from her self-imposed cocoon, she slipped off with Robert to be married, and the happy couple fled to France, where she penned an apologetic letter to her rudely abandoned father. Mr. Barrett was understandably angry, and although she continued to write him pleading letters for many years, he did not even break the seal to read them.

Elizabeth and Robert moved on to Italy, where they lived rapturously on money she inherited from her grandmother, supplemented by a smaller allowance that Robert received from his still-living father. I don't like that! Robert

Browning had somewhat timorously offered to get a job, but E.B.B. decided that he should devote himself totally to his Muse and probably to her. He was therefore content to let his wife and father support him; and the elder Mr. Browning, who had worked hard all his life as a bank employee to obtain his modest means, was apparently happy to do so.

So unsuccessful was Robert's early poetry that Elizabeth's fame and fortune far exceeded his, until she died at the age of fifty-five in his arms. Only after her passing did he begin to produce some of the world's greatest poetry. Now, a century later, Robert is classed with England's immortals, while Elizabeth is chiefly remembered for a few of the love sonnets she wrote to him. Could Robert's delayed recognition have been because of Elizabeth's gentle domination of him during her lifetime?

True, their love was abiding, but until John Kenyon (Dr. A. J. Armstrong?) left them an inheritance they could scarcely have supported themselves without assistance from the elder Browning. And had they not achieved their happiness at the emotional expense of Mr. Barrett (Lily), Elizabeth's stern and unforgiving, but previously doting father?

Yet, much as I tried to defend Lily as Mr. Barrett in my objectivity, I had to concede that he had warts and flaws. The Guides had praised him as the high-minded Savonarola, and they called him "a noble soul" in the French incarnation. Why, then, in the English incarnation should he derive his wealth principally from slaves in Jamaica?

I posed this question to the Guides, and after referring to the pledges each soul supposedly makes before returning to physcial body, they surprisingly wrote: "He returned to free mankind of its shackles and prove to himself that he was capable of assisting others to treat all men as equals." Supposedly, then, Lily had deliberately chosen to be born into a family of rich slaveholders in order to help free slaves.

Next they wrote: "Without the intervening French life Lily would doubtless have made the grade in the English embodiment. But having tasted pleasure and affluence in the France of Louis XV, he felt the need for money and comfort, and that reduced his drive for freeing the slaves who helped produce his income. Because of this blot on his character he sank lower, until even his children became slaves to his ego. Not a pretty scene, and for this reason Lily will not again incarnate until he has worked it out here, for he does not dare risk another physical round of succumbing to temptations. He wishes to regain the purity of soul he attained in Florence and even in France, where he was a ready helper for all who touched his life.

"This he will achieve, for a more brilliant light shines forth from him now than when first we saw him here. Perhaps confession is indeed good for the soul! Having discussed the error of his ways at these morning sessions, and sought through you to help others mend their ways, he has purged himself and will attain far higher realms."

This brought to mind something Arthur Ford had written in *A World Beyond:* that although progress can be more rapid in physical embodiment because of the hurdles to overcome, it is also possible to advance in the spirit state. What the Guides now seemed to be saying was that the rate of progress can be accelerated on "the other side" if souls are willing to work through earth people to right wrongs. This ability comes only when a soul, after passing to spirit, has reviewed his last incarnation and noted all of his mistakes. Then he must learn to forgive himself as well as others.

"To err is human, to forgive divine."

Afterword

Each time that we reenter physical body we come as lonely strangers, but we encounter self over and over and old friends along the way. Each of us is as an island in a storm-tossed sea, until we eventually win release and discover true union with loved ones on the other side of the door called death. Some are rich and famous in one life, poor and humble in another, but always we are pilgrims climbing toward the mountain peak and ultimate reunion with our Creator. How hard the climb and how high the barriers depend solely on us. We have no one to blame except ourselves.

Keenly aware of my own limitations, faults, and foibles, I asked the Guides if they would tell me about some other lives when I was especially wicked or had a very rough time, in order to give more balance to the book. They replied:

"There were no such lives that you shared with Arthur Ford or Lily, so we feel that they are not a part of this book. There were times when you were less proper and times of greater poverty, yes, although we feel that they are affecting you less in this incarnation than those lives we have told to you. Grinding poverty is no menace. It is the way a soul reacts to the situation that establishes the gain or the loss in character. Some waywardness does not leave as black a mark on one's soul record as heedlessness and selfishness, so forget it and move onward and upward in the determination to see God."

Edgar Cayce said that few souls can work on the karma from more than three or four lives in any single incarnation, and my spirit friends had now provided ten for me to chew on. One more than a cat! Musing on these remarkable stories, and squirming uncomfortably as I thought of my purported sins of commission and omission, I asked the Guides what purpose is served by knowing about reincarnation. They replied with some questions of their own:

"If we lived only one life and the end came with death, would there be any particular value in being ethical, honest, and loving? We live in an ethical society, yes, but what recompense would there be for helping others and praying for grace if at the moment of death the world forever ceased for us? What if through negligence or ill will we made a dire error that caused great harm to someone else? Even if there were eternal life in the spirit, would we not be damned through eternity for a single act we deeply regret? How would we repay that grievous error if judgment awaited us after a single life in the flesh?

"This is why it is so important to be able to return again and again, carrying with us our resolution to undo previous harm by paying for it in self and so improving the lot of others that we atone for that wrong. If everyone remembered the pledge he made before entering physical body and worked ceaselessly to undo wrong that had previously been committed, we would have no need to recall previous lives. Perfection would be achieved.

"But what of those who in the hurly-burly of living recall nothing, simply setting about the task of amassing money and getting ahead? They will probably go on committing the same errors. That's why it's important to pause, take stock of all that is affecting the present life, and consciously set about to reform one's ways. If we should recall that in a previous life we abandoned our children, let's say, would we not then in this life seek endlessly to shelter little strays and improve the lot of youngsters? If the crippled leg in this life was the result of having purposely injured another's leg in times gone by, would we not then welcome this opportunity to make amends, rather than complain about the bad luck that turned us into a cripple? The same with the blind or the deaf or those with other handicaps. (The Biblical eye for an eye, tooth for a tooth.)

"How opportune to pay back in a physical lifetime, which is but a fleeting moment, if by so doing we wipe out the blot and move that much nearer to reunion with our Creator. Meditation unlocks the door to our subconscious, where our memory bank is stored, and by daily meditation we can find the key."

Perhaps Lily has been overcompensating in his attempt to justify himself. At any rate, the Guides used him to illustrate a significant point they wished to make, writing: "Savonarola was a remarkable person who walked with God in his mysticism, yet felt such burning wrath for the pope of those last days and the wrongs of the Church hierarchy that he took it upon himself to reform the world of Florence and Rome. Within him burned the flame of righteousness, and his soul was dedicated to freeing men from the shackles of bad faith in both temporal and secular affairs.

"His purity of heart and love for humanity kindled that flame in the hearts of others, and when it became impossible for him to continue in obedience to the derelict pope who did not speak with the voice of God, he endured excommunication from the faith of his fathers. Rather than make his peace with powers he felt to be wrong, he went to his death as a martyr. Small wonder, then, that he held rigidly to his own beliefs and views as the father of the Barrett household in England. Stern he was, and somewhat dictatorial, but loving and wise in the ways of obedience to the Creator. Truth he worshiped, and the freedom to worship. Let all who read these words remember that each of us has been, through other lives, a many-faceted soul. Some of the sides sparkle more brilliantly than others, but we can gradually round off the corners until we become as a perfect sphere, lighting the way for all who are yet to be returned to physical form."

Continuing their poetic analogy, they wrote: "Our purpose is to sparkle so brilliantly that like an array of candles, we vanquish the gloom and light the path with such luminescence that others will more easily find their way. To each of us is given the same opportunity to cast a light in the gloom. Whether rich or poor, obscure or famous, young or old, we are presented almost daily with opportunities to choose good over evil, right over wrong, strength over weakness, and to offer a steadying hand to someone else. With each correct choice we take another leap forward in our progress toward perfection, while with the wrong choice we sink backward in confusion. The race will be won when all of us are as pilgrims, each serving as a strong right hand to the other. Comrades in arms, pulling together, we will lighten the load and become filled with joyousness, for joy will become the music of eternity."

Joy—the music of eternity! I envied the Guides that graceful turn of phrase. Perhaps those words would have been an effective way to close this book, but there was something else I wanted to know. Many have asked why, if we return again and again to physical life, there are so many more people in the world today than ever before in recorded history? Where did all these souls come from?

Edgar Cayce said the earth's population was greater during Atlantean days than now, and the Guides have indicated that the earth was more overcrowded at the time of Mu and Atlantis than today. Now they introduced still another explanation, writing:

"Each soul in physical form today has had numerous

earth lives, for if one at this stage of existence came into physical being for the first time, he would be virtually unable to cope with the complications of today's so-called civilization. All souls were created simultaneously at the beginning of time, but some have never entered physical form, some only seldom, and others frequently. The challenges of earth form are so exhilarating that some love to rush forth to battle, while others hang back, fearful of succumbing to temptations that would slow their reunion with God.

"Either way, it is a toughening and strengthening of the center core, and because of the diversities of experiences, each soul adds something to the entirety. Some profit greatly by physical life, and others to a lesser degree, but all are moving toward that perfection which all have craved since separation from the Creator. Each soul determines how rapid his progression will be by act, word, and thought, each day and year. We are our own judges, and what we think at each moment helps to mold the course that will be ours throughout eternity. Helping others lightens our own load."

The Guides seemed to be saying that there is no paucity of souls and that many who had not chosen to reincarnate since the time of Mu and Atlantis have come back during the current century, perhaps attracted by a civilization which most clearly resembles the one they knew. In the 1930's Edgar Cayce predicted that large numbers of Atlanteans would be returning shortly, because of the unique opportunities at this particular time for advancing science and invention. And he warned of dire trouble ahead because many of these souls were ones who, through evil activity, had managed to destroy the advanced civilization of Atlantis. Now the Guides were pointing out that there are still countless spirits who have never yet incarnated, but who may choose to enter the earth at some more peaceful, less complicated period.

In concluding their comments on Group Karma, the Guides made this observation: "Nearly every lifetime shows some advancement toward the ultimate goal, unless a soul so succumbs to evil, as Hitler did, that he plunges backward into the dark pit of spiritual torment for long periods of anguish. Unless we are exceedingly careful in our daily conduct, we are all in danger of taking backward steps which will have to be regained in future advancements.

"Remember: What we think, we become. Think kindly thoughts, and that is the person you will be. Think negatively or unkindly of others, and you will drag down self to lower levels."

Jesus said, "Love thy neighbor as thyself." This is the key to the open door that leads to reunion with God.